DIVINATIONS: REREADING LATE ANCIENT RELIGION

Series Editors: Daniel Boyarin, Virginia Burrus, Derek Krueger

A Traveling Homeland

The Babylonian Talmud as Diaspora

Daniel Boyarin

PENN

UNIVERSITY OF PENNSYLVANIA PRESS

PHILADELPHIA

Publication of this volume was aided by a generous grant
from the Andrew W. Mellon Foundation.

Published by
University of Pennsylvania Press
Philadelphia, Pennsylvania 19104-4112
www.upenn.edu/pennpress

Printed in the United States of America on acid-free paper
1 3 5 7 9 10 8 6 4 2

A Cataloging-in-Publication record is available from the Library of Congress

Boyarin, Daniel, author.
A traveling homeland : the Babylonian Talmud as diasporia / Daniel Boyarin
pages cm. — (Divinations: rereading late ancient religion
Includes bibliographical references and index.
ISBN 978-0-8122-4724-4 (alk. paper)
1. Jewish diaspora. 2. Talmud. I. Title. II. Series: Divinations
DS134.B675 2015
909'.04924—dc23

2015005397

Dedicated to the memory of my teacher
and master, Prof. Hayyim Zalman Dimitrovsky

May the memory of the righteous be for a blessing

והתלמוד אני שם על דברי מקום מולד וארץ המכורות.

I set the Talmud at the head of all my words
as a birthplace and land of origin.

—Rabbi Shmuel Hanagid, Spain, eleventh century

Contents

Prelude

A Different Diaspora

> What is there worth saving and holding on to between the extremes of exile on the one hand, and the often bloody-minded affirmations of nationalism on the other?[1] Daniel Boyarin answers, of course: Diaspora.

From the *Chabad* [Hassidic group] *Journal*, May 7, 2013:

> Editor's Note:
>
> Dear Friend,
> Jerusalem is never far from our minds. After all, it is there that creation began, and it has been the center of our national devotion for 3,000 years. Three times a day, we face Jerusalem as we pray for the return of Gd's presence to His holy city.
>
> Over 150 years ago, there was a pious and devoted Jew who desired to apply himself to Torah study and prayer in the Holy Land. When he shared his plan with his rebbe, Rabbi Menachem Mendel of Lubavitch, he was taken aback by the rebbe's response, "Make Israel here." He did not need to go to Israel; rather, he was to bring Israel where he lived.

Every time we do another mitzvah, we port a bit of Jerusalem to wherever we are. And when the word is full of such mini-Jerusalems, we will all gather in our homeland—for real.

Menachem Posner,
on behalf of the Chabad.org Editorial Team

Khachig Tölölyan has written beautifully of what it is that makes a diaspora:

The diasporist project, as C. L. R. James understood, is to enhance the articulations between the past and present, homeland and hostland segments of the transnation. . . . [W]ithout such connections—however sporadic and discontinuous they may be in arduous practice—to claim that the individual diasporan is a member of the diaspora and that the diasporic segment is a part of the homeland people (which can consist of the descendants of shared ancestors from three or ten generations ago) risks mere biologism. This pitfall can be juxtaposed with the mere psychologism that regards diaspora to be the figure of boundary-crossing multiplicity and links a specific individual to that diaspora by virtue of the multiplicity they share and—again—of birth. A diaspora is never merely an accident of birth, a clump of individuals living outside their ancestral homeland, each with a hybrid subjectivity, lacking collective practices that underscore (not just) their difference from others, but also their similarity to each other, and their links to the people on the homeland. Without some such minimum stringency of definition, most of America—or Argentina, or New Zealand, or any modern immigrant-nation—would just as easily be a diaspora. Perhaps diasporists should and must aspire to teach every nation, especially those created by immigration, to see and honor the diasporas within, to transform

> their/our self-perception and self-representation. But if we wish to remake the nations of the world in the image of the diaspora, we will not do it by fiats of redefinition, one person at a time.[2]

Revisioning "Diaspora"

Despite the correct observation just cited from Tölölyan, redefining things can sometimes be the beginning of a new political vision, so let us begin. Generally, the term "diaspora" with respect to Jews is used in one of three acceptations, which are not mutually exclusive.

It can appear in a kind of timeless geographical sense: the Jews who do not dwell in Palestine, whatever their historical conditions. So, for instance, all the thriving communities of Jews throughout the Ottoman Empire and beyond would be called the Diaspora, in contrast to a small, if vital, community of refugee Jews from Spain who have landed in Palestine in the sixteenth century, simply owing to geographical location. Second, it can appear in a chronological sense, the Diaspora being understood as a one-time event of scattering from the "homeland."[3] Third, in a lachrymose sense, it can be the condition of being an oppressed minority longing to go "home."[4]

Thus, for instance, in discussing the broadening of the usage of "diaspora" to refer to Africans, Armenians, and Irish, Robin Cohen writes: "With the Jews, these peoples conceived their scattering as arising from a cataclysmic event that had traumatized the group as a whole, thereby creating the central historical experience of victimhood at the hands of a cruel oppressor."[5] Cohen, to be sure, complicates this as a controlling definition for diaspora *tout court* but leaves it essentially in place as an adequate description of the situation of the Jews, and that is precisely where the current intervention takes place.

I am proposing a very different approach to the question of diaspora: namely, diaspora as a particular kind of cultural hybridity and as a mode of analysis rather than as an essential thing.[6] As shown by the analysis of the narrative of the four captives, with which I begin Chapter 1, diaspora is most usefully mobilized as a synchronic condition by which human groups are related to one another in space; they may, and frequently do, have an origin in an actually shared past but need not and, moreover, need not even have a story of such a shared—traumatic—past.

Cohen allows for such a component, writing that "diasporas often *mobilize a collective identity*, not only a place of settlement or only in respect of an imagined, putative or real homeland, but also *in solidarity with co-ethnic members in other countries*. Bonds of language, religion, culture and a sense of a common fate impregnate such a transnational relationship and give to it an affective, intimate quality that formal citizenship or long settlement frequently lack. A useful description of this sentiment is 'co-responsibility.'"[7] I am inclined to agree with Cohen, while taking much more seriously than he does the element of shared culture; but I would promote this from a marginal to an essential aspect of the description of a diaspora. Cohen further writes that "in some limited circumstances the term *'diaspora' can be used to describe transnational bonds of co-responsibility even where historically exclusive territorial claims are not strongly articulated*."[8]

In the present book, I claim that this is not only a better way of describing the historical experiences of the Jews (of some Jews and not at all marginal ones) but has to be a defining feature of diaspora as a taxon to distinguish that term from others—migration, exile, displacement—with which it is frequently conflated. As Cohen notes, there have been various challenges to the notion of diaspora, owing to its putative association with notions of "origin" and "homeland," on the one hand, and on the other, because "in this formulation [diaspora], the primary orientation and attachment of diasporic populations is to their homelands and cultures."[9] The point of the current argument is to displace these notions of diaspora, maintaining its value and utility for describing particular kinds of cultural practice and solidarity without disputing the existence of others.

Once this is said, a homeland, real or even imagined, is not a necessary or sufficient condition for the existence of a diaspora. In the history of a given collective, there can be multiple diasporas, from Babylonia, Bari and Otranto, Spain, and the Rhineland—shifting homelands, and even diaspora in which homeland is entirely absent and replaced by cultural connection.[10] While trauma is frequently a point of origin or concomitant of diasporic existence, trauma is neither necessary nor sufficient to constitute a diaspora. Robin Cohen writes: "While the increased complexity and deterritorialization of identities are valid phenomena and constitutive of a small minority of diasporas (generally those that had been doubly or multiply displaced over time), ideas of home and often the stronger inflection of homeland remain powerful discourses."[11] Not so minor, perhaps, as Cohen imagines; what I want to show is that crucial moments of Jewish historical experience fit this "minority" description much better than traditional ways of conceiving the Jewish diaspora.

Introducing the Argument

This book begins with an idea that is not new: that in some deep sense, a book has been the portable homeland of the Jewish people. The title of the book recalls Heine, who may have been the first to deploy this topos. More recent writers who have reflected it include George Steiner, Simon Schama, and my own departed teacher, Prof. Hayyim Zalman Dimitrovsky, ז"ל. What I try to do in this book is to work out the particulars and the implications of that powerful notion in greater historical and theoretical detail than anyone has attempted until now, to the best of my knowledge. If, indeed, the Talmud is the/a homeland of the Jews, what does that say about the historical and theoretical description of the Jews as a diaspora? First, the book explores some of the actual textual practices within and around the Talmud that make the topos more than a pretty metaphor; second, it queries (or rather, I query through its agency) what difference that makes for thinking diaspora as a theoretical/

historical category for understanding the history of the Jews, as well as contexts broader than that of the Jewish people. On the first of these issues, I will try to show how the Talmud constructs through its own textual practice a diaspora according to a precise definition offered in Chapter 1, and I will argue that those very textual practices subtended a further set of practices around the Talmud until nearly the present (or even beyond it), which further maintained a diasporic existence. In other words, I suggest that the Talmud is a diasporist text that engenders diasporic existence and practice. On the second issue, I will suggest how these specifications might add to a robustly reconfigured notion of "diaspora" and ways that it can usefully be distinguished from some other closely related terms of art.

"Diaspora," in its original sense, while founded on a Greek word meaning "scattering" and thus implying some sort of a point of origin, unlike "exile,"[12] frequently focuses more on the creation of new homes and not on not being at home.[13] Indeed, the Septuagint uses a mixture of positive and negative terms, παροικία (sojourning), μετοικεσία (captivity), ἀποικία (colony) for the Hebrew גולה—usually translated "exile"—and never "diaspora."[14] As Unnik concludes, the translators of the Septuagint "inscribed their situation not as 'Exile' but as something else."[15] According to Unnik, the "something else" was, nonetheless, generally negatively charged.[16] However, even in Hebrew/Aramaic, this term גולה is not always negatively charged. Thus the Rabbis can say: "Be a *goleh* to a place of Torah!"[17] As we will see Chapter 1, that is how they frequently understood the move to Babylonia: as a move to a better place, where the Torah could be studied more easily. We cannot think of the Jewish diaspora, therefore, as always and everywhere being understood as a forced and oppressive exile. Of Philo, historian Steve Mason has remarked: "Putting Judaeans on the same level as Romans or early Greek monarchies, he speaks of what we nowadays call 'the Jewish diaspora'—a term signifying dislocation and possibly distress—as rather a positive *colonization*: the colonies abroad [ἀποικίαι] in other prosperous lands preserve the customs of the mother-city."[18]

It is time, once and for all, to dispose of the false etymology that interprets diaspora as the "scattering of male seed," and thus, eo ipso, masculinist. The Greek verb *speirein*, from which it is derived, means "to scatter," and it does frequently carry the senses of "to scatter seed" and "to procreate" (for males) (incidentally giving the lie to Stefan Helmreich's claim, repeated by Robin Cohen, that this "scattering of seed" is somehow a uniquely Judaeo-Christian and Islamic metaphor), but this has no bearing on the meaning of *diaspeirein* in the Greek of the Septuagint, which has nary a hint of such interpretations. Helmreich's conclusion from his false etymologizing that "[d]iaspora, in its traditional sense, thus refers us to a system of kinship reckoned through men and suggests the questions of legitimacy in paternity that patriarchy generates"[19] is beyond science fiction and into the realm of fantasy. As Johannes Tromp makes clear, the meaning of the verb is originally simply "to spread," without any further connotations. Nothing in the formation or use of the verb *diaspeirein* (apparently a Septuagintal neologism)[20] implies planting, seeding, sowing, or male ejaculation. Jewish diaspora certainly was masculinist, as we shall see, but there is nothing in the etymology of the term that makes it semantically necessary that it be so.[21]

Initially, it would seem, the verb simply referred to the spread-out nature of the people. However, as Tromp makes clear, it carries as well a further and much more sinister connotation: the scattering of the defeated enemy. The god, as defender of his people, causes their enemies to scatter before him and them. When the god is angered, he causes his people to scatter before the enemies.[22] Given this fraught set of meanings *ab origine*, it is no wonder that later, the term "diaspora," derived from this verb, would carry a variety of affective connotations as well.

In the chapters that follow, I will explore one particular Jewish diaspora (for, as we can divine, a diaspora is not one): the one produced by the Babylonian Talmud. The Talmud produces diaspora in three ways, corresponding to my three chapters below. In Chapter 2, "At Home in Babylonia: The Talmud as Diasporist Manifesto," I will show how the

Talmud imagines its own community, how it projects its being in Babylonia, its raison d'être, the status of Palestine, and its own status vis-à-vis Palestine as well. I will argue that multiple passages in the Talmud add up to a virtual diasporist manifesto, acknowledging that there are other much less sanguine voices to be found also. This controversy is thematized in the Talmud in the practice and discourse of different Rabbis.

In Chapter 3, "In the Land of Talmud: The Textual Making of a Diasporic Folk," several examples of analysis of talmudic texts are undertaken to show how the talmudic sugya (sustained dialectical engagement with a particular issue) is constructed seamlessly but highly significantly out of Palestinian and Babylonian materials constructing the two geographically dispersed collectives as dwellers in one place, the Land of Talmud. It is in this chapter, the longest, that the main argument for diaspora as doubled cultural location is pursued.

In Chapter 4, "Looking for Our Routes; or, the Talmud and the Making of Diasporas: Sefarad and Ashkenaz," the argument shifts gears, demonstrating the ongoing productivity of the doubled (bifocal) cultural production produced by the Talmud as it traverses different times and climes, the methods of its study ever developing via contact with circumambient culture and moving on to other Jewish collectives in other places where other cultural discourses become incorporated into and affected by talmudic learning.

Following my revered teacher to whose memory this volume is dedicated, Prof. Hayyim Zalman Dimitrovsky, I argue that it is the talmudic study itself that has constituted the Jewish people as a diaspora.

Chapter 1

Diaspora and the Jewish Diasporas

> Any theoretical formulation is ultimately a bid for changing the way we think, rather than a putative revelation from a higher order of knowledge.
>
> —Jonathan Boyarin

> Where once there were dispersions, there now is diaspora.
>
> —Khachig Tölölyan[1]

A famous[2] story preserved in a medieval chronicle, *The Book of Tradition*, by Abraham Ibn Daud (1110–c. 1180), narrates the origins of a Jewish diaspora in the western Muslim world via the pirate capture of a ship bearing four great Talmud scholars. Since its most recent editor and scholarly commentator, the late Gerson D. Cohen, has demonstrated almost beyond a shadow of a doubt that the story is entirely fictive, we can learn from it a great deal of truth.[3] Regarding the expansion of the number of castaways from three found in Ibn Daud's apparent sources to four,[4] Cohen remarks: "Ibn Daud could very logically extend the homily by pointing to the four scholars who initiated the salvation and spread of Torah among the Jews of the Muslim world after the eclipse of Jewish learning in Babylonia. In other words, four is the number symbolic of divine providence over Israel, and the four captives are truly the new dispersion, despatched by God to the four corners of the earth, as it were, to bring the word of the Torah into the new and last stage of the fourth kingdom."[5] Without accepting or denying Cohen's apocalyptic interpretation, I firmly assent to his assertion that the making of the story to be about four scholars dispersed to four places (with one scholar and his place admitted by the author as completely unknown to himself and thus heightening its symbolic nature) makes this a story of a new dispersion, a new diaspora, and thus germane for my inquiry into the meaning of Jewish diaspora(s) and their relevance for the study of diaspora tout court.

Sailing from Byzantium

Let's have a look at Ibn Daud's story.[6] Ibn Daud begins by remarking that the income that had formerly come to the Babylonian academies from "the Maghreb, Ifriqiya, Egypt, and the Holy Land" was discontinued, owing to the following circumstance. The half-millennium-old Babylonian Jewish community had founded a series of great talmudic academies having their beginnings in the third century AD.[7] Initially entirely nurtured from Palestinian rabbinic teachers and Babylonians who had traveled there and brought "Torah" back with them, these academies quickly took on an independent stature, as full partners and then successors of the Palestinian academies. They remained vital long after the Palestinian center had been effectively destroyed in the fifth century, and they retained their power into the tenth century. This, then, is the legend of their demise. A fleet of conquest sent by the Muslim ruler of Cordova to capture Christian ships sailed to the Ionian Sea, where "they encountered a ship carrying four great scholars, who were traveling from the city of Bari to a city called Sefastin, and who were on their way to a Kallah convention." The destination city seems to be made up, but the institution of the Kallah (a month-long mass Talmud study session) was very much a Babylonian one, and, as Cohen remarks,

"Ibn Daud assumes, of course, that his reader will understand how close a connection there was between Kallah conventions and the income of the academies."[8] With fine insight, Cohen also remarks on the irony that the men's [*sic*] proposal to attend the ingathering at Babylonia and presumably continue the support of the academies there is met by God's disposal: the dispersion of these scholars among the western communities and their declaration of independence from the Babylonians.[9]

The four scholars, at any rate, were R. Ḥushiel, father of Rabbenu Ḥananel; Rabbi Moses; R. Shemariah, son of R. Elḥanan; and "as for the fourth, I do not know his name." Rabbi Moses, traveling en famille, loses his wife when the captain of the boat wished to violate her "as she was exceedingly beautiful," and she chose death (having been promised entry into the next world) rather than dishonor and threw herself into the sea and drowned: "The commander wanted to violate R. Moses' wife, inasmuch as she was exceedingly beautiful. Thereupon, she cried out in Hebrew to her husband, R. Moses, and asked him whether those who drown in the sea will be quickened at the time of the resurrection of the dead. He replied unto her: 'The Lord said: I will bring them back from Bashan; I will bring them back from the depths of the sea' (Ps. 68:23). Having heard his reply, she cast herself into the sea and drowned."

That is the end of this tragic incident for Ibn Daud (but not for us; we will return to it later). The story moves right along. Not having revealed to the commander that they were, in fact, important talmudic scholars, they are all redeemed individually by different Jewish communities, in accord with the mitzvah to redeem captives: Rabbi Shemariah was sold in Alexandria and ended up in Fustat (Cairo), where he became head of the academy in the place that eventually Maimonides would call home. Rabbi Ḥushiel was sold in Kairawan in Tunisia, where he begat his son Rabbenu Ḥananel, who wrote the first great commentary on the Talmud (this bit, at any rate, is not fiction; we talmudists study this commentary to this day). As for the fourth anonymous rabbi, we could at least imagine him as having reached the Rhineland, whose Jewish communities and talmudic learning were founded then by Jews who came from southern Italy in the tenth and eleventh centuries.[10] Rabbi Moses ends up in Cordova, where, as thematized outright in the story, now wifeless, he replaces the dependence of that community on the Babylonian center with his own learning and teaching; they will neither depend on or support the Babylonian academies, for now they have knowledge of the Babylonian book:

> Then the commander arrived at Cordova where he sold R. Moses along with R. Ḥanokh. He was redeemed by the people of Cordova, who were under the impression that he was a man of no education. Now there was in Cordova a synagogue that was called the Synagogue of the Academy,[11] where a judge by the name of R. Nathan the Pious, who was a man of distinction, used to preside. However, the people of Spain were not thoroughly versed in the words of our Rabbis, of blessed memory. Nevertheless, with the little knowledge they did possess, they were conducting a school and interpreting constantly.[12] [Once] R. Nathan explained [the law requiring] "immersion [of the finger] for each sprinkling," which is found in the tractate Yoma, but he was unable to explain it correctly. Thereupon, R. Moses, who was seated in the corner like an attendant, arose before R. Nathan and said to him: "Rabbi, this would result in an excess of immersions." When he and the students heard his words, they marveled to each other and asked him to explain the law to them. This he did quite properly. Then each of them propounded to him all the difficulties which they had, and he replied to them out of the abundance of his wisdom. Outside the School there were litigants who were not permitted to enter until the students had completed their lesson. On that day, R. Nathan the judge walked out, and the litigants went after him. However, he said to them: "I am no longer judge. This man, who is garbed in rags and is a stranger, is my master, and I shall be his disciple from this day

> on. You ought to appoint him judge of the community of Cordova." And that is exactly what they did. The community then assigned him a large stipend and honored him with costly garments and a carriage. [At that point,] the commander wished to retract his sale. However, the King would not permit him to do so, for he was delighted by the fact that the Jews of his domain no longer had need of the people of Babylonia.[13]

It can hardly be missed, and hardly has been, that this legend repeats in almost every detail the legend of Hillel's coming from Babylonia, demonstrating his greater learning of the Palestinian Pharisaic tradition and being deferred to by the Pharisaic leaders at the time, the Sons of Bathyra, founding, thereby, the Hillelite academy:

> Our Sages have taught: The halakha was unknown to the Sons of Bathyra [the previous leaders of the Jewish community in Palestine]. Once the fourteenth of Nisan fell on a Sabbath, and they had forgotten and did not know whether the Passover sacrifice was offered on the Sabbath or not. They said: Is there anyone who knows whether the Passover sacrifice supersedes Sabbath or not? They said to them: there is one person who arrived here from Babylonia, and his name is Hillel the Babylonian, and he was a disciple of the two giants of the generation, Shemaia and Abtalyon, who knows whether the Passover sacrifice supersedes Sabbath or not. (Pesaḥim 66a; and see Bava Meṣia 85a)

Indeed, he did know, and they put him in charge of the yeshiva over, and instead of, the Sons of Bathyra, and he founded a dynasty that stood for four hundred years. In other words, just as in the Talmud we have a foundation legend of the Hillelite yeshiva, we have in the story of the four captive rabbis a foundation legend of the major centers of talmudic learning and hence rabbanite and rabbinic hegemony in the medieval western and southern Mediterranean.[14] It is not inapposite to mark one big difference between the source text and its echo; in the original classical rabbinic story, the question asked was of great practical halakhic importance, while here it couldn't be of less practical matter, as it pertains to the form of a ceremony in the Temple, destroyed a millennium earlier.[15] It is the fact of learning the Talmud, not always its actual halakhic content, that is important.

Gerson Cohen has pointed to a crucial point in this narrative: "Surely the attentive reader of Sefer ha-Qabbalah could not have failed to notice that in the whole history of Jewish oral tradition, which is the prime subject of Ibn Daud's tract, these four scholars were the only ones, with the exception of the first Moses, who had not 'received' their authority from a recognized predecessor."[16] While Cohen clearly understands this narrative as marking a shift in the location of authority from the East (Babylonia) to the West (Spain and the Maghreb), he also adumbrates the point that the very mode of authority has shifted too: "What Ibn Daud wants to tell us is that R. Moses' arrival in Spain—and of R. Ḥushiel in Kairawan and of R. Shemariah in Cairo—marks the transition to a new era in Jewish learning, the era of the Rabbinate. The arrival of the 'four' captives in their respective new homes spells the end of the gaonate and hegemony of Babylonia and, on the other hand, the beginning of learning the world over."[17] This is even more significant in the context of Ibn Daud's book, which, as an anti-Karaite polemic, seeks to persuade readers of the orderly transfer of rabbinic, Babylonian talmudic, authority. Let me dwell on this point momentarily. The Karaite movement, which arose in the ninth century, denied the significance of oral tradition and insisted that all authority was vested in the written Torah. In a work combating that "heretical" movement, Ibn Daud nonetheless insists that what had been previously invested in transmission from teacher to student and from the central authorities to peripheries is now, Ibn Daud is saying, invested in book learning, in the book of the oral tradition, and it is this cultural connection via the book that constitutes the Talmud as diaspora.[18] The book is now the homeland and the center.

The shift from the authority of the academies to the authority of the book, symbolized by the fact that these rabbis were sailing from the Adriatic Coast and not Babylonia, is thus doubly significant. What is not emphasized enough in Cohen's account is that it is not only an institutional shift but an entirely new form of culture and discourse, from a local (Babylonian) to a trans-local, dispersed, diasporic cultural form. In Cairo, Cordova, Kairawan, and the unnamed fourth place, it is now the common possession of the book, the Talmud, that constitutes legitimacy: Rabbi Moses claimed his authority by being able to interpret the Talmud correctly; Rabbi Ḥushiel's greatest achievement was to beget the author of the first great Talmud commentary. The network of communities that possess this text constitute the new diaspora. That text is, of course, the *Babylonian* Talmud, the very text that originated in the Land that they no longer need.

At the same time, let me not neglect to mention that it is not only (or even not so much) the written book that has been transmitted but also the ability to interpret it. The Talmud is a cryptic book, and without commentary—that is, without teachers—it is nearly impenetrable. Hence even though the Jews of Cordova already had the book, as is made manifest in the story, they needed Rabbi Moses to open it up for them.[19] The narrative, by marking explicitly the fact that the Cordovans already had the text of the Talmud but did not know how to interpret it until their new teacher arrived from Bari, provides a pointed answer to Rav Hai Gaon, who, in the eleventh century, polemicized with the Kairawan Jews, who, according to him, had access to the written Talmud but did not know how to interpret it.[20] Ibn Daud is letting us know that the two alternatives are not Babylonian geonic authority or autodidactic chaos. The book and its correct modes of interpretation are equally subject to traveling and settling down—knowledge of the Talmud's correct interpretation had traveled from Byzantium and settled in Cordova, Cairo, and Kairawan. The traveling book, picking up modes of interpretation and traveling with them where these modes were further developed locally and transported further, becomes the homeland for medieval Jewry.

Babylonia had been the homeland for a diaspora—figured most dramatically in the alleged dependence of the "Holy Land" on the Babylonian Sages—but is no longer. The new diaspora needs no center, since the Talmud in writing and its interpreting sages have been planted in the new diaspora from southern Italy. The mutual having of the text of diaspora and diasporist text, the Babylonian Talmud, constitutes the communities of the West as their own diaspora. The traveling and shared book has become the homeland for these Jewish communities and ultimately for all Israel. As my teacher the lamented H. Z. Dimitrovsky, to whose memory this volume is dedicated, has lyrically written: "The period from the beginning of the eleventh century and until the time when the world of Talmud ceased to be the world of the Jewish people . . . in its content, its spirit, and its tendencies, is a period in which the Talmud is the center of the world of the Jew."[21] A diaspora constituted by a book and its culture, not a lost homeland. The end of that period to which Dimitrovsky alludes is sometime around the nineteenth century and even later. Indeed, as Cohen does not fail to remark, Ibn Daud even concludes that from now on, Torah—read: the Babylonian Talmud and its interpretation—would have to travel from Spain to Babylonia.[22]

Shlomo Ibn Gabirol (c. 1021–c. 1058) extols Rabbi Shmuel Hannagid, born in Cordova (993–1055): "His responsa are read in Babylonia and discussed by the heads of the congregations, and it is as if Rav Hai [the great leader of the Babylonian academy] does not exist before him."[23] There is thus a concerted move by the new Sefardi center that displaces the Babylonian one (and ultimately the Italian one) and becomes the new center. Similarly, only a couple of generations later, we find the Jewish sages of Siponto, just a short journey up the coast (ninety-eight kilometers) from Bari, appealing to the commentary of Rabbenu Ḥananel to settle their great confusions about the laws of kashrut.[24] It is not so much the era of the rabbinate that this story enacts but the era of the Talmud as the traveling homeland—replacing Babylonia—of the Jews (some Jews, at any rate).

This text theorizes and represents diaspora in a very different way from how we are used to thinking of it. Indeed, it emblematizes willy-nilly nearly all the interventions that I wish to make in this book into the conceptualization of diaspora.[25] First, there is no center. These rabbis were traveling from Byzantium toward Babylonia (if Cohen's compelling interpretation is correct) when they were captured and sold by privateers. The location from which they were scattered was not Palestine, not even Babylonia, but Bari on the Adriatic Sea, of which the great twelfth-century northern French Rabbenu Tam would say: "For from Bari goes out Torah, and the word of God from Otranto," appropriating/diasporizing the biblical "For from Zion goes out Torah, and the word of God from Jerusalem."[26] (For the further diasporic adventures of this saying, see below.)

Second, this story is not a record of trauma. The "catastrophe" here is the capture of the ship. This figures the sometimes, but not always and not necessarily, traumatic or even forced aspect of scattering; even in this story, the scattering of these rabbis is only productive, not in any way traumatic for them—for the male protagonists, at any rate (not a small qualification; see below). I am not claiming that diaspora representations are never records of trauma, not in the Jewish or any other situation; they most frequently are. I am suggesting that trauma and oppression are not necessary or the most useful of taxa for describing diasporic situations. Many traumatic dispersions and situations of oppression have simply not issued in diasporas in any meaningful sense; there are, as increasingly recognized, diasporic cultural formations (including some of the Jews') that were formed not out of trauma but voluntary migration for many other purposes or even simply produced out of secondary connections between scattered communities.[27]

Third, this new diaspora is a diaspora constituted by the learning of the book—the Babylonian Talmud, which they bring with them—but not even from its "source" or point of "origin" but from Byzantine Italy, where its learning was already established.[28] Diaspora follows diaspora; the center does not hold, and the book becomes the center.[29]

Fourth, and most important, this diaspora is constructed as a discursive/cultural practice among already existing and thriving Jewish communities, not as a natural consequence of some traumatic founding event.[30] These communities of Jews exist and thrive before they are constituted as diasporic with respect to one another. Instead of the various communities all turning to the Babylonian academies, a series of connections between periphery and one center, now they are connected with one another. The Babylonian Talmud replaces Babylon, which has replaced Palestine as the homeland; the ties that bind this diaspora together are synchronic, their common culture of the study of this book and the language, modes of thought, and practice that come with it.

Highly illuminating comparisons can be made to the usage of "diaspora" in the study of the cultural connections of people of African descent in the world. A nice example of such a synchronically constructed diaspora is cited by Martin Baumann. Referring to the twentieth century, he writes: "Long established 'Black communities' outside the African continent became renamed as diasporas. A unity of those once enslaved thus was and is constructed; a mythical relation of all overseas 'Blacks' with an idealized 'Africa' arose; and politically, former and present power relations were pointed out and questioned."[31] Brent Hayes Edwards even more usefully articulates what it is that constructs these alliances as diasporic: their shared cultural practice: "Of course, black artists and intellectuals, from Edward Wilmot Blyden, Martin Delany, and Pauline Hopkins in the nineteenth century to W. E. B. Du Bois, Marcus Garvey, and Tiemoko Garan Kouyaté in the early twentieth, have long been engaged with themes of internationalism, but *diaspora* has only in the past forty years been a term of choice to express the links and commonalities among groups of African descent throughout the world."[32]

One of the most important aspects of the history of African diaspora is that the object, Africa, is clearly and avowedly a construct. African descended people around the world did not come from a place called "Africa" but from Dahomey, the Camaroons, Ghana, Ivory Coast, and so on (some of these names are anachronistic), places of distinct historical and cultural identities. As Du Bois famously wrote: "The idea of one Africa to unite the thought and ideals of all native peoples of the dark continent belongs to the twentieth century and stems naturally from the West Indies and the United States. Here various groups of Africans, quite separate in origin, became so united in experience and so exposed to the impact of new cultures that they began to think of Africa as one idea and one land."[33] We can observe a close analogy to the ideas concretized in the narrative of the four captives: the making in time of a diaspora as a cultural production. It matters not for Jewish culture whether the Land of Israel as origin is a similar construct; what is important is that the diaspora is produced in real time out of the narratives of such an originary land and out of the current robust cultural connections sustained, in part, by that narrative.

Among diaspora theorists, another Cohen—Robin—has made a major advance over previous scholars[34] in pointing to the collective identity formation mobilized by diasporas: "not only a place of settlement or only in respect of an imagined, putative or real homeland, but also *in solidarity with co-ethnic members in other countries.*"[35] Cohen has realized that this implies that there need not be a traumatic dispersal from a particular homeland to constitute a diaspora—indeed, there could be what he calls "deterritorialized diaspora." I want to build on Cohen but treat the deterritorialized diaspora not as a special case or exceptional form of diaspora but rather as its ideal type. I propose once more that diaspora be understood as a synchronic cultural situation applicable to people who participate in a doubled cultural (and frequently linguistic) location, in which they share a culture with the place in which they dwell but also with another group of people who live elsewhere, in which they have a local and a trans-local cultural identity and expression at the same time.[36] None of this needs imply trauma, an original scene of forced dispersion, a longing for a homeland, or even the existence of a myth of one homeland. Finbarr Flood's comments on the Islamic *umma* are certainly apposite here:

> The idea of mobility is, however, intrinsic to the history and prescriptions of Islam, a religion whose year zero is measured not from the birth of the Prophet but from the migration of the nascent Muslim community from Mecca to Medina. Moreover, the duty to make the pilgrimage to Mecca at least once in a lifetime imbues Islam with an institution that is global in its extent and impact, not least on the circulation of artistic concepts and forms. Without entailing a deterritorialized concept of identity, the need to negotiate between the local and the trans-local, the lived experience of the quotidian and the ideal of the umma, an imagined community with a global reach, has been a distinguishing figure of Islamic cultures from their inception.[37]

Although Flood does not use the terminology of "diaspora" here, it is that sense of a negotiation of local and trans-local that marks my interpretation of Ibn Daud and of Jewish diaspora more broadly in this book. Note that the word *umma* is the same word that Jewish Arab writers use to describe their people/peoplehood.[38] Obviously, a Muslim *umma* in a diaspora comprising Spaniards, Arabs, Persians, Chinese, and Indonesians is a diaspora that has come into being through cultural and religious contacts, not one that has been, traumatically or not, scattered from a putative originary homeland. There should be no mistake: Mecca is not the homeland that produces this diaspora, any more than there are connections with people "back home." Mecca is the Holy City, and pilgrimage there is the practice that enables the doubled location of the communities of the *umma*, including their shared artistic practices, which are then located in two contexts/locations: the trans-local Islamic one; and the local traditions and conditions of artistic practice.

Think, for instance, of Turkish and Persian Islamic art: it is these doubled and shared practices that would inspire me to refer to the *umma* as a diaspora. Similarly, for the medieval Jewish diaspora, as for the Babylonian Talmud, Jerusalem remains, of course, the Holy City and the Land of Israel the Holy Land, but in no meaningful sense is it a homeland; certainly, there may be no connection with folks "back home" from the early Middle Ages on.[39] These two concepts need better delineation, especially within the study of Jews and their histories; in truth, neither is necessary to account for a diaspora. What renders Jewry diasporic are the connections with other Jews in other places all over the world, owing to common cultural discourses and practices, primarily the study of Talmud. This comparison with the *umma* bears out the usefulness of my assertion that the best way to conceive of diaspora is as a synchronic condition in which a given collective is oriented twice: once toward the place that they are in, and once toward another place—once toward a local culture, and once toward a culture that they share with other related collectives that are not in their place.[40]

Ibn Daud is a perfect example of such a double orientation. On the one hand, as we've seen, he was the great champion of traditional talmudic learning and the prophet of its spread in his Arabic-speaking world. On the other hand, he was the figure who introduced Aristotelianism and the philosophy of Avicenna into Jewish culture. Not only that but "he continues to attract the attention of scholars of Latin philosophy, too, since there are indications that our Ibn Daud is the Avendauth who cooperated with Dominicus Gundissalinus in translating philosophical texts from Arabic into Latin."[41] The dual orientation of his cultural commitments, to the trans-local talmudic study and to the philosophical culture of Arabic and Latin Spain, marks Ibn Daud as the perfect figure of diaspora.[42] Similarly, Hannagid and his panegyricist, Ibn Gabirol, are perfect figures of diasporic culture: Hannagid, in addition to being a great talmudist and Hebrew poet, was appointed vizier in Spain and general of the armies in 1027; Ibn Gabirol is known better in Europe as Avicebron, author of the great Neoplatonist allegorical poem *Fons Vitae*, and even thought there to have been a Christian until the nineteenth century.

Why Did Rabbi Moses Lose His Wife?; or, Did Jewish Women Have a Diaspora?

There is someone whom we might seem to be forgetting. As remarked above, one protagonist of Ibn Daud's story does suffer trauma. I mean, of course, Rabbi Moses' wife, who drowned herself to avoid sexual violation. What is the meaning of Ibn Daud's inclusion of this seemingly otiose and certainly odious detail in his story? This raises the question of whether, on the grounds of the notion of diaspora toward which I am working, Jewish women (or underclass Jews) have ever had a diaspora. There is a sense in which the current interrogation and reconfiguring of accounts of Jewish diaspora focuses this question even more intensely than more traditional accounts. If previous accounts of diaspora as traumatic include women, since they were participants in that trauma as well, my revisionist description of diaspora as not necessarily traumatic and essentially as a mode of cultural productivity apparently leaves women completely out of, at least this, diaspora as figured in the narrative.[43]

Comparing the narrative of the suicide of Rabbi Moses' wife that we read above with its source will bring this point home. In the Talmud, we read what was almost certainly the model for Ibn Daud's story. Fascinatingly, it begins with a reading of the first verses of Psalm 137:

> Said Rav Yehuda in the name of Rav: What is it that is written, "By the waters of Babylon, there we sat down, and there we wept when we remembered Zion"? It teaches that God showed King David (who authored this psalm via prophecy) the first destruction and the second destruction. The first destruction, as it is written, "By the waters of Babylon, there we sat down, and there we wept when we remembered Zion," and the second destruction, as it is written, "Remember, O LORD, the children of Edom in the day of Jerusalem, who said, raze it, raze it, even to the foundation thereof (Edom being understood as Rome)."

> Rav Yehuda in the name of Shmuel, and there are those who say Rabbi Ammi, and some say it was taught in a tannaitic [early rabbinic, prior to the third-century Mishna] source: There was an incident of four hundred boys and girls who were captured for shame [to be used sexually]. They perceived why they had been taken. They said, "If we drown in the sea, will we come into the next world?" The greatest of them interpreted: Said the Lord, From Bashan I will return them; I will return them from the depths of the sea [Ps. 68:23]. "From Bashan I will return them" from between the teeth of lions [taking Bashan in a punning way as *ben shinei*, or between the teeth]. "From the depths of the sea," those are the ones who drown in the sea. When the girls heard this, they all jumped and fell into the sea. The boys drew an a fortiori argument and said: These for whom being penetrated is their "way" did so; we for whom being penetrated is not our way, even more so and even more! They also jumped into the sea. On these [boys and girls,] the Scripture says: For you we are killed all the day, we have been as sheep to the slaughter. (Ps. 44:23) (Gittin 57b)[44]

There may be little question but that Ibn Daud is using this story, as proven by use of the same verse from Psalms 68. Indeed, for the learned readers of his narrative, this notorious passage from the Talmud would be called to mind as an intertext. For Gerson Cohen, this source for Ibn Daud serves as further evidence that the medieval author made up his story of the four captives from whole cloth (or rather, felted it together with scraps of recycled cloth).[45] The argument is certainly compelling but does not go nearly far enough. While giving us Ibn Daud's source, it does not explain why he chose to incorporate this particular detail into his narrative, nor does it come close to understanding the enormous differences between the source and target texts, with respect to the question of gender, for, notwithstanding the sexist and homophobic elements in the putative source text, both males and females kill themselves to preserve their chastity, while in Ibn Daud, it is only a woman who does so.[46] In a sense, this could be taken as a figure for the translation of diaspora from trauma, which at least binds men and women in death, to a culturally productive mode in which males, as it were, sow the seeds of talmudic learning.[47]

Let me emphasize this point once more. Since Ibn Daud has clearly composed his narrative of the four captive rabbis out of a bricolage from various earlier rabbinic narratives, his choice of details is especially significant; since this is not quite fiction in our sense of prose literature for pleasure but a composed founding legend fraught with purport, one can't say that the detail is there only to provide narrative interest (such as this might be). The story has been transformed from a representation of the piety of young Israelites, both male and female, to one in which a woman, the only woman in the story, dies.[48] One could perhaps say that in the transition from a story of trauma into a story of triumph, matters have gotten worse for the females.

Given these considerations, I suggest that this story figures how gender functions in the production of *this* diaspora—namely, the absence of women from this story. It is not only that Rabbi Moses' wife is disappeared on the way but *his* young son, Ḥanokh, survives and becomes the next leader of the Cordovan community. Ḥushiel, moreover, who arrives at Kairawan alone, somehow begets the great Rabbenu Ḥananel without any mention of female intervention at all.[49] All this figures the ways that this kind of diaspora, the diaspora of talmudic learning, is exclusionary with respect to gender—and yes, to class, as well. Rabbi Moses lost his wife, clearly a learned and pious woman (she could speak to him in Hebrew and understand his midrashic answer) because this realm of diasporic culture is only for learned men.

We must attend to the complexity of the narrative that derives, or constitutes its power, not only from the overt positive lessons it delivers but from additional, less than "ideal," layers. Rabbi Moses' masculine boundaries are violated and compromised. This is the price that has to be paid for the dissemination(!) of talmudic learning. It's also part of the larger picture of captivity, of dehumanizing the rabbinic figures (qua captives). From a Lévi-Straussian perspective, the death of the wife would mean, inter alia, that a new cultural identity is formed, based on no kinship relationship with the East.[50]

In Chapter 4, I attempt to address the questions of gender raised by this book and its theorization of diaspora.

"The" Jews and the Diaspora Question

We can take away five points from the above discussions:

1. There is not one Jewish diaspora but many; diasporas from Palestine, from Babylonia, from southern Italy, from Spain, from Lithuania (to Palestine). It is impossible to assume or predict that all these experiences were the same.
2. While there may be, and frequently is, trauma associated with diasporic movements, it is not trauma that is constitutive of diaspora for Jews.
3. Jewish communities in diaspora are not necessarily suffering and oppressed communities.
4. A diaspora can be produced out of already existing communities by the production of new cultural ties and connections.
5. It is precisely those common cultural practices that constitute the multiple collectives as a diaspora.

I am going to argue that these five claims, as substantiated below, lead to a reevaluation of the meaning of diaspora in Jewish history but allow us to revise our understanding of the heuristic value of the concept "diaspora" tout court. To misappropriate the quotation from Tölölyan that I cited as a motto to this chapter: where once there was diaspora, now there are diasporas. Earlier in the present critical moment, there were attempts to essentialize and define precisely and normatively of what a diaspora consists (who is in and who is out). In his germinal paper for modern diaspora theory, William Safran has offered the following definition:

> I suggest that . . . the concept of diaspora be applied to expatriate minority communities whose members share several of the following characteristics: 1) they, or their ancestors, have been dispersed from a specific original "center" to two or more "peripheral," or foreign, regions; 2) they retain a collective memory, vision, or myth about their original homeland—its physical location, history, and achievements; 3) they believe that they are not—and perhaps cannot be—fully accepted by their host society and therefore feel partly alienated and insulated from it; 4) they regard their ancestral homeland as their true, ideal home and as the place to which they or their descendants would (or should) eventually return—when conditions are appropriate; 5) they believe that they should, collectively, be committed to the maintenance or restoration of their original homeland and to its safety and prosperity; and 6) they continue to relate, personally or vicariously, to that homeland in one way or another, and their ethno-communal consciousness and solidarity are importantly defined by the existence of such a relationship. In terms of that definition, we may legitimately speak of the Armenian, Maghrebi, Turkish, Palestinian, Cuban, Greek, and perhaps Chinese diasporas at present and of the Polish diaspora of the past, although none of them fully conforms to the "ideal type" of the Jewish Diaspora.[51]

What is remarkable about these definitions (aside from the fact that they do not hold up) is the claim that the Jewish diaspora is an "ideal type." Recently, Rogers Brubaker has explored this theme more explicitly:

> Most early discussions of diaspora were firmly rooted in a conceptual "homeland"; they were concerned with a paradigmatic case, or a small number of core cases. The paradigmatic case was, of course, the Jewish diaspora; some dictionary definitions of diaspora, until recently, did not simply illustrate but defined the word with reference to that case (Sheffer 2003, p. 9). As discussions of diasporas began to branch out to include other cases, they remained oriented, at least initially, to this conceptual homeland—to the Jewish case and the other "classical" diasporas, Armenian and Greek. When historian George Shepperson introduced the notion of the African diaspora, for example, he did so by expressly engaging the Jewish experience (Shepperson 1966; Alpers 2001; Edwards 2001). The Palestinian diaspora, too, has been construed as a "catastrophic" diaspora—or in Cohen's (1997) term, a "victim diaspora"—on the model of the Jewish case. The concept of the trading diaspora—or in John Armstrong's (1976) terms, the "mobilized diaspora"—was constructed on the model of another aspect of the Jewish, as well as the Greek and Armenian, experience. Chinese, Indians, Lebanese, Baltic Germans and the Hausa of Nigeria are among those often mentioned as trading diasporas. An orientation to these paradigmatic cases informs some influential recent discussions as well, including those of Safran (1991), Clifford (1994), and Cohen (1997). As Clifford put it, "we should be able to recognize the strong entailment of Jewish history on the language of diaspora without making that history a definitive model. Jewish (and Greek and Armenian) diasporas can be taken as non-normative starting points for a discourse that is traveling or hybridizing in new global conditions" (1994, p. 306).[52]

These attempts are partly an effort to reclaim the name "diaspora," if not—certainly not—for the Jews alone, then for a specific sort of historical situation, rescuing it from its latter-day trendiness, which has threatened to dissolve the term into nothingness.[53] As Martin Baumann, along with others, has remarked:

> The semantic broadening of "diaspora," both in terms of relating it to any dispersed group of people and to conceptualize a certain type of consciousness, have made "diaspora" one of the most fashionable terms in academic discourse of late 20th century. Authors and writers use the once restricted notion in an arbitrary, unspecified, fairly free way. Apparently, an often plainly metaphorical application of "diaspora" is prevalent, encompassing under the very term a wide range of phenomena considered appropriate. The term's popularity has resulted in a dissolution of semantics, "decomposing" into exactly the early Greek philosophical meaning the notion's ability to encompass certain situations and relations.[54]

If the term "diaspora" needs to be rescued to maintain some kind of specificity, we would do well to attend carefully to the historical specificities of historical communities. I know something about Jews.

One of the greatest difficulties with most accounts of Jewish diaspora is that they are ahistorical, treating diaspora as an essence—almost a Platonic idea—and refusing to pay attention to the ever-changing and developing conditions of Jewish life through time and space.[55] Thus Robin Cohen writes with respect to the psalm "By the waters of Babylon, we sat down and wept when we remembered thee, O Sion": "The loneliness and sadness of the diasporic experience of the Jews is poignantly evoked in this psalm. . . . Such evocations are common."[56]

Cohen does his best to complicate this picture, but the very terms of this initial statement render his job of nuancing extremely difficult, if not impossible. His very assumption or positing of "the diasporic experience of the Jews" is the problem, and starting off with such terminology, conceptual apparatus, renders a solution very distant. While he recognizes, for instance, that "Jewish migratory experiences were much more diverse and more complex than the catastrophic tradition allows," he indicts his critical task as to "interrogate and supersede the Jewish tradition"[57] rather than to interrogate whether his account of the Jewish tradition is accurate. He further compounds the difficulty by making unsupported statements such as "'diaspora' evolved as the preferred and catch-all expression covering sin, scattering, emigration and the possibilities of repentance and return."[58] Among which Jews? At what time? In which language(s)? The word doesn't even exist, of course, in Hebrew or Yiddish; and in the Septuagint, it is not used as the translation equivalent of *gola* or *galut*.[59] As Baumann observes in explaining that the Septuagint does not translate the Hebrew terms for "exile" by "diaspora":

> In retrospect, post-Babylonian Jews theologically interpreted the Babylonian captivity as God's punishment for their disobedience to the commands of the Torah. With the return to Palestine and Jerusalem in the late sixth century BCE, this punishment had come to an end. Living outside the "Holy Land" subsequently—that is, from the fifth century BCE on —was understood differently. It was not an imposed punishment for breaking the laws of God. It involved no "deportation" as denoted by the Hebrew terms *gola* and *galut*. These terms were translated in the Septuagint by αἰχμαλωσία (*aichmalosía*, captivity by war), μετοικεσία (*metoikesía*, moving under force), and other terms [but not diaspora].[60]

Cohen even delivers himself of the startling pronouncement that "Babylon subsequently became a codeword among Jews . . . for the afflictions, isolation and insecurity of living in a foreign place, set adrift, cut off from their roots and their sense of identity, oppressed by an alien ruling class."[61] This statement simply ignores the fact that only in one particular type of Jewish literature is this even somewhat the case—namely, Apocalyptic (4 Ezra, Revelation, Bob Marley), while in rabbinic texts, to the best of my knowledge, "Babylon" never functions in this sense.[62] More startling, we discover that "[o]ne narrative, promoted often by Zionists and religious leaders in the tradition of Ezra and the prophets, depicts the Babylonian and Sephardi experiences as a wholly negative process of deracination."[63] Come again. Are we to understand that the religious leaders rejected the Babylonian Talmud as well as the rabbinic literature and liturgical poetry of the Spanish Jews, owing to the religious leaders' alleged allegiance to the Babylonian Ezra? Given this absolute straw man, Cohen sets out to suggest a "revisionist view of Babylon," but it seems that it is only his view that needs revisioning, not some putative Jewish tradition that needs superseding.[64]

I cite and criticize Cohen here, perhaps too harshly, not because he is exceptional in usage of the alleged experience of the Jews in theorizing diaspora but because he is all too typical of such efforts. On the one hand, we have writers such as Safran and his ilk, who seek to define Jewish diaspora essentialistically (and in accord with what is essentially Zionist ideology) and use it as a regulating gate check for the legitimacy of applying the term to others. On the other hand, we have those who, accepting the same definitions of Jewish diaspora, seek to define Jewish experience as not being diasporic (or not diasporic enough) because it, in the form of a mythical eternal Zionism, seeks only to return "home" and, in Stuart Hall's memorable phrase, to drive the indigenes into the sea.[65] Zionism, which is the privation of diaspora, the avowed enemy of diasporic Jewishness,[66] is taken as the essential affirmation and description of historical Jewish experience, which is then named as not diasporic and foreordained for supersession.[67] Cohen's is, arguably, the best of the lot and, therefore, necessitates the kind of critique that I have offered here.

What I argue is that Jewish diaspora, like that of blacks as evoked by Gilroy, cannot be reversed, although it can be dissipated and destroyed. Given the regulating force of Jewish diaspora, whether "ideal type" or model to be superseded, it becomes clear why it is so important to get the Jewish diaspora right—some version of right and not one that is descriptively, manifestly untrue with respect to the historical or literary record. Just as for black folk, "in a transnational circuit, then, articulation offers the means to account for the diversity of black 'takes' on diaspora, which Hall himself explicitly begins to theorize in the late 1980s as a frame of cultural identity determined not through 'return' but through difference: 'not by essence or purity' but by the recognition of a necessary heterogeneity and diversity; by a conception of 'identity' which lives with and through, not despite, difference,"[68] so, too, for Jewfolk. Just as, according to Edwards, diaspora was mobilized with regard to black studies "to break with a depoliticizing emphasis on 'unity' and unidirectional return in midcentury black internationalist scholarship," such has been its use in Jewish discourse as well. I could say with Edwards, mutatis mutandis: "I am rethinking the uses of *diaspora* more precisely to compel a discussion of the *politics of nominalization*, in a moment of prolixity and careless rhetoric when such a question is often the first casualty. An intellectual history of the term is needed, in other words, because *diaspora* is taken up at a particular conjuncture in black scholarly discourse to do a particular kind of epistemological work."[69]

Revisioning Diaspora

In this little book, I will argue that the Jewish diaspora has been seriously misdescribed by most theoreticians and historians until now and that when more accurately interpreted, the Jewish historical experience serves as an excellent example—not regulating norm or even ideal type—of what seems to me is most useful in identifying diaspora and constraining the term sufficiently so that it is a useful taxonomic term for discussing modes of cultural hybridity. Tölölyan, in a highly important programmatic essay several years ago, wrote: "The setting aside of the pre-1968 meanings of 'diaspora' is not in itself a fundamental problem: meanings change. The amnesia concerning these changes is a problem; so is the ease with which 'diaspora' is now used as a synonym for related phenomena until recently covered by distinct terms like expatriate, exile, ethnic, minority, refugee, migrant, sojourner and overseas community."[70] I agree with Tölölyan and wish to reclaim diaspora as a specific term but without making one particular community's experience definitive.

Safran used his highly politicized understanding of the Jewish diasporic experience to simply define out of diaspora other communities that didn't fit his own criteria, based on his understanding of that Jewish experience as he—along with myriad others—has chosen to define that experience.[71] Beyond the initial criterion—which is, in a sense, analytically necessary—namely, dispersion, none of the rest of the definition is necessary, or even, as it will be my task to show in this book, necessarily characteristic of that "ideal type" of diaspora, that of the Jews. Neither diachronic forced dispersion nor political inequality nor a lack of cultural autonomy constitutes a putatively unified Jewish experience of diaspora. It is not so much, I will suggest, that Safran's terms are wrong, whatever that might mean, but that there is within Jewish culture itself, within the classic instance of diaspora, the Jews of Babylonia, an entirely different self-understanding, on the one hand—and a set of cultural practices, those produced and defined by the Babylonian Talmud, that belie those terms.[72] The Talmud in its textual practices produces Babylonia as a homeland, and, since this Babylonia is produced by a text that can move, that homeland becomes portable and reproduces itself over and over. The Talmud, I would submit, is not only the only classical work of the rabbinic period produced outside the Land of Israel; it is a diasporist manifesto, Diasporist Manifesto Number 1.

Chapter 2

At Home in Babylonia: The Talmud as Diasporist Manifesto

> It has not yet been sufficiently proven that the preservation of the national character of the Jews outside their land is connected with the Land of the Jews. On the contrary; in the ancient sources, there appear clear echoes of a strong feeling of intellectual and religious non-dependence and independence [אי תלות ועצמאות], which was dominant among the Babylonian Jews.
>
> —Hayyim Zalman Dimitrovsky[1]

The Babylonian Talmud is, I propose, the diasporist text of the Rabbis, par excellence. The Babylonian Talmud produces thematically the image of diaspora that would ultimately project it as the text of diaspora throughout later Jewish history. Moulie Vidas has pointed out how the Talmud theorizes the Diaspora: "Immigration to Palestine becomes unnecessary as the Talmud legitimizes exile; the hegemony of the Land of Israel as the ultimate destination for Jews becomes irrelevant. The action the Bavli takes with respect to geographical matters is similar to the one it took with respect to ethnic matters: it decentralizes the Jewish world not only genealogically but geographically by allowing multiple communities."[2] The Babylonian Talmud thematizes this perspective in more than one way.

Several times, we hear tell of a particularly important synagogue in the town of Nehardea, called by the somewhat bizarre name בי כנישתא דשף ויתיב, "The Synagogue That Slid and Settled." Already by the early Byzantine era if not before that time, an etymology had been offered for the name of this highly important synagogue: that it had slid from its place in Palestine and settled in Babylonia.[3] With the exile of Jeconia in 597 BC, the Jews took with them stones and sand from the destroyed Temple in Jerusalem and used them to build their synagogue in Babylonia. According to the Talmud, this synagogue was where the Shekhina dwelled in Babylonia. Babylon replaces Palestine, and this synagogue is the new Temple, albeit a reduced one, a מקדש מעט, which, as Elḥanan Reiner has pointed out, is not mere metaphor. A striking text from the late geonic[4] period evinces this point in the context of an argument of one of the last geonim for maintaining the absolute primacy of the Babylonian center over-against the new ones in the West, as figured in the story of the four captives, discussed in Chapter 1:

> Several matters support this: The legacy of the parents is the merit of the ancestors [the parents leave to their children their own merits; that is, my illustrious ancestors render me worthy to be the leader of the Jews worldwide]. And also the place [where it is said] that the Shekhina removed to Babylonia provides support, as it is said: "For your sake, I sent to Babylonia" [Isa. 43:14], and the Sages interpreted: Beloved is Israel that in any place to which they are removed, the Shekhina is with them. And now she is in Babylonia, standing on her foundation, as it is written: O Zion, save yourself, O dweller with the daughter of Babylon [Zech. 2:7=11, in Hebrew]. Behold the Talmud testifies to you [when it asks]: In Babylon, where is the Shekhina? Rav said, in the synagogue of Hutzal; and Shmuel said, in the Synagogue That Slid and Settled in Nehardea. And don't say that it is [only] here or [only] there, but sometimes it is here and sometimes there. And there [in Babylon],

> the yeshiva is established to augment the Shekhina. They bless always also in the Synagogue the Prophet Ezekiel and Daniel the greatly beloved and Ezra the Scribe and Barukh ben Neria and the rest of the Sages of the Talmud [all Babylonian Jewish luminaries], the memory of all of them for a blessing.[5]

One of the last of the geonim,[6] the leaders of the Babylonian yeshivot, defends here the proposition that Babylonia is the Holy Land—that the Divine Presence, the Shekhina, came with them to Babylonia, settled there (like the synagogue itself), and established it as a new Holy Land.[7] Zion is now in Babylon, and detaching from Babylon is detaching from the Holy Land. The proof from Zechariah is brilliant. Simply from the fact that "Zion" personified as the Shekhina is called "dweller with the Daughter of Babylon," we see that the Shekhina moved with the Jews to that place and dwelled there and made it holy. He finishes off his peroration by listing a selection of Babylonian Jewish holy men going back to Ezekiel and Jeremiah's scribe and forward to the men who produced the Talmud. In indicating that the Shekhina, the Divine Presence in the world, came with them to Babylonia and established herself in a holy place there, the Talmud and its Babylonian rabbinic tradents[8] are reorienting our sense of what a diaspora is, providing us with a new conception of diaspora, transforming it in our conceptual apparatus from a contrast between center and periphery, from homeland and exile, to a process of the establishment of ever-new centers and locating it in cultural practice—not ancient trauma or loss. It is the study—the yeshiva—that augments the presence of the Shekhina in Babylonia. The legend of the building of this synagogue out of actual sand and stones brought by Jeconia from the Temple in Jerusalem renders graphic the status of this building as a new Temple.

In a brilliant and riveting analysis of this tradition as well as another one concerning the Synagogue of Ezekiel, Reiner has shown that the ideological point of these stories is to separate the founding of the Babylonian Jewish community entirely from the destruction of the Temple. Jeconia, the king, was captured and brought to Babylonia a decade before the destruction, kept in prison until after the destruction, and then released in Babylonia. Replacing the narrative significance of the destruction of the Temple, we have instead, as Reiner demonstrates, a founding legend in which the trauma of the captivity is separated from that Palestinian trauma and redeemed, as it were, by the release of the king, who then founds the community in Babylonia, together with the prophet Ezekiel: king and high priest. The synagogue in Babylonia is thus a new Temple, and the community a new Land of Israel.[9]

Going back a bit further in time than this post-talmudic Babylonian rabbinic text, we can see similar thoughts occurring to the Talmud, using this same verse: "Rav Yehuda said: Anyone who lives in Babylonia, it is as if he lives in Palestine, as it says, 'O Zion, save yourself, O dweller with the daughter of Babylon.'"[10] The same reasoning is applied here: the verses render Zion equivalent to the "dweller with the daughter of Babylon," so that dweller is equal to Zion. To be sure, in the geonic text, it is the Shekhina that is understood as the referent of Zion, while in the talmudic text, it is the individual Israelite. Let me take a step backward and place this statement in the context of diaspora theory.

In an influential programmatic essay, Richard Marienstras has distinguished between modern notions of diaspora and that of the Jews: "But it is only recently that this term has come to describe minority groups whose awareness of their identity is defined by a relationship, territorially discontinuous, with a group settled 'elsewhere' (for example: the Chinese diaspora, the Corsican diaspora in Mainland France etc.)." So far, so good, but then he goes on to explicitly exclude the Jews from such definitions: "Historically the term described the dispersed Jewish communities, that is those not living in *Eretz Israel*." True enough, but why, then, does he assert that "'Diaspora' presumes that there exists an independent or heavily populated Jewish political centre"?[11] For most of Jewish history, that is simply and inarguably not the case. Was there no Jewish diaspora from 63 BC until AD 1948? My contention is that the Babylonian Talmud falsifies the very ways that the Jewish diaspora is taken as a positive or negative ideal type of diaspora. Robin Cohen—along with most authorities—continues to stress the allegedly traumatic nature of diaspora, using the Jewish experience as paradigmatic. In writing of the addition of the dispersion of Africans, Armenians, and Irish to the Jews in the category of diaspora, he insists: "These scarring historical calamities—Babylon for the Jews, slavery for the Africans, massacres and forced displacement for the Armenians, famine for the Irish and the formation of the state of Israel for the Palestinians—lend a particular colouring to these five diasporas. . . . [T]heir victim origin is either self-affirmed or accepted by outside observers as determining their *predominant* character."[12] Cohen maintains that whatever criteria we wish to assert for an account of the "common features of a diaspora," "*the traumatic dispersal from an original homeland* and *the salience of the homeland in the collective memory of a forcibly dispersed group*" are sine qua nons.[13] This is, one might suggest, the lachrymose version of what makes a diaspora—precisely what I have set out to displace here.[14]

I am not, of course, claiming that such a representation is not to be found among historical Jews. Perhaps the most salient literary model for this depiction of the meaning of diaspora is Psalm 137:[15]

> [1]By the rivers of Babylon, there we sat down, yea, we wept,
> when we remembered Zion. [2]We hanged our harps upon the
> willows in the midst thereof. [3]For there they that carried us
> away captive required of us a song; and they that wasted us
> required of us mirth, saying, Sing us one of the songs of Zion.
> [4]How shall we sing the Lord's song in a strange land? [5]If I for-
> get thee, O Jerusalem, let my right hand forget her cunning. [6]If
> I do not remember thee, let my tongue cleave to the roof of my
> mouth; if I prefer not Jerusalem above my chief joy. [7]Remem-
> ber, O Lord, the children of Edom in the day of Jerusalem;
> who said, Raze it, raze it, even to the foundation thereof. [8]O
> daughter of Babylon, who art to be destroyed; happy shall he
> be, that rewardeth thee as thou hast served us. Happy shall he
> be, that taketh and dasheth thy little ones against the stones.

This text, it could be said, has been made definitive of modern Zionist understanding of diaspora (including, at least in some quarters, the bloodthirsty ending, especially on the day known today in Israel and other Zionist circles as "the Day of Jerusalem"). I do not wish to suggest that this understanding of Jewish life in Babylonia disappeared from talmudic culture entirely. We certainly find such texts as:

> For the sins of sexual immorality, idol worship, and ignoring the fallow and Jubilee years, exile comes into the world, and they are exiled, and others come and settle in their place, for it says, "For the inhabitants of the Land have done all these abominations [Leviticus 18]," and it is written, "And the Land will become impure and I will demand its revenge," and it is written, "that the Land will not vomit you in your defiling of it," and with respect to idol worship, it is written, "and I will put your corpses . . .," and it is written, "and I will destroy your temples . . ., and you I will disperse among the nations. With respect to the fallow and Jubilee years, it says, "Then the Land will desire its Sabbaths, all the days of barrenness, and you will be in the land of your enemies," and it is written, "all the days of the barrenness, it will rest [have its Sabbath]." (Shabbat 33a)

While this entirely negative representation of dwelling in Babylon holds for certain times and places for the Babylonian diaspora of the Jews and, of course, for multiple later Jewish diasporas as well, it is hardly the case that this is a universal self-understanding by the Babylonian Jews through the millennium (and more) of their life there, nor has it been the experience of many other Jewish communities.

As Isaiah Gafni has remarked: "In rabbinic eyes, however, past and present tend to coalesce, and thus in time the rabbinic community of Babylonia would point to those earliest biblical days of captivity as the first links in an unbroken chain of enhanced Jewish existence 'by the rivers of Babylon,' claiming that all the requisite trappings of a vital and self-sufficient community were transported from Jerusalem to Babylon even prior to the destruction of the First Temple."[16] As such, a sense of trauma or even discomfort is falsified as a necessary condition for the existence of a diaspora by the very historical experience of the putatively prototype diaspora, that of the Jews, as a set of universally applicable criteria for the identification of diasporas or the definition of diaspora as a thing. Surely, by the time of the Babylonian Talmud, the lachrymosity was a thing of the past.

Even while recognizing that Jews had been sent into exile in Babylon, the Talmud can figure that occurrence as a positive event and even as a homecoming in the following remarkable text (Pesaḥim 87b): "And Rabbi El'azar[17] said: The Holy Blessed One only exiled Israel among the nations in order that converts will be added to them. As it says, 'And I sowed her in the land' [Hos. 2:25]. Does a person ever sow a peck except to harvest several bushels?"

We see here Rabbi El'azar focusing not on the scattering, but on the sowing, of seeds, the productivity that issues from the scattering of Israel among the nations. This rabbinic view is much closer in sensibility to the views of Jews such as Josephus and Philo, who consider the purpose of the diaspora of the Jews not as punishment and not as suffering but to fulfill their universal task of spreading the knowledge of the One God throughout the world. According to other views in the sequel to this passage, the Jews were sent to Sasanian lands in order to protect them.

> Rabbi 'Oshaya said: What is it that is written "even the Righteous acts toward the inhabitants of his villages in Israel [פרזונו בישראל]" (Judg. 5:11). The Holy Blessed One acted righteously toward Israel by scattering [פזרנון] them among the nations. And this is identical to what a certain sectarian [מין] said to Rabbi Yehuda Nesi'a:[18] "We are superior to you, for it says of you: 'For six months did Joab remain there with all Israel, until he had cut off every male in Edom' (1 Kings 11:16), but you have been among us for many years and we have not done

anything to you."[19] He said to him [the sectarian]: "If you will, one of the students will answer you." Rabbi ʿOshaya answered him: "That's because you didn't know what to do. If you wanted to kill all of us, but [you couldn't because] we're not all among you, and if you killed those who are among you, they would call you a cut-off kingdom!" He said to him, "By the Agape of Rome [Isis!],[20] that's what we think about when we get up and when we lie down."

The diaspora of Israel, according to this view, was an act of righteousness, justice cum charity to Israel; for by scattering them, the likelihood of them all being exterminated by one ruler is lessened. This point is illustrated, then, by the narrative of the conversation that Rabbi Yehuda Nesi'a (the fourth-century Patriarch in Palestine) held with a certain "sectarian." The sectarian challenged the Rabbi, claiming moral superiority over the Jews, for it says that in the time of King David, Joab and all Israel remained in Edom until they had killed all the males, but the Jews have been living among the Romans (Edom) for many years and have been left alone. The Rabbi answers that this is not owing to their moral superiority but to the advantage that Israel has by living under more than one rule, so that they cannot all be exterminated, in any case.[21] The sectarian grants that this is indeed their dilemma and the reason that they do not harm Israel. The only plausible "candidate" for this position of "sectarian" is Rome, for only this entity has Jews both inside and outside it. The statement adds up to the claim that by being dispersed outside the Roman Empire into the Sasanian one, the Jews have been, in effect, saved from genocide.

A partial parallel to this text from another place in the Talmud makes its point even clearer. With respect to a certain Roman minister described as being righteous, the Talmud asks:

What is the story of Qaṭia bar Shalom? There was a certain Caesar, who hated the Jews. He asked the important men of

> the kingdom: If one develops a boil on his leg, shall he amputate it and live, or leave it and suffer? They said to him, "He should cut it off and live." But Qaṭia bar Shalom said to him: "First of all, you won't be able [to kill] all of them, for it says, 'Behold, like the four winds of heaven I have scattered them [Zech. 2:6].' What did he say? If he [God, the speaker of the prophetic verse] had meant that he had scattered them to the four winds, why does he say, 'like the four winds'? It should have said, 'to the four winds'! Rather [to teach us] that just as the world cannot exist without the four winds, so the world cannot exist without Israel, and second, they will call you a cut-off empire."[22] (Avoda Zara 10b)

First, the name of the Roman official is clearly emblematic. Literally, it means "Cut off, the Son of Peace." This name will take on further resonance later in the story, when "Cut off" circumcised himself as he is being led to be executed by the same Caesar; but right now, his name is clearly being referred to when he says, "They will call you a cut-off empire."[23] Now note that this statement about "cut-off empire" makes literary sense in the context here in Avoda Zara in a way that quite eludes us in Pesaḥim. A diachronic approach—sources and influences, so to speak—would say that the story in Pesaḥim has simply and somewhat awkwardly taken over material from the story in Avoda Zara (and that may make literary historical sense in its own right), but as Riffaterre has taught us and as Zvi Septimus so richly developed and articulated, such "ungrammaticalities" (Riffaterre's term)[24] or "trigger words" (Septimus's),[25] the use of rare words or collocations in two or more passages of the Talmud signal synchronically to readers to read them together to allow them to enrich each other's import. Taken together, their common enhanced theme is the greater security afforded to Israel by not being entirely encompassed within the Roman Empire, as a Caesar who hates the Jews and regards them as a boil on the empire cannot possibly exterminate them, since many of their number are in Persian lands.

This is not an after-the-fact consolation or apologetic for the diaspora but a full-fledged approbation of it on the part of the Babylonian Talmud, as we will see further.

This point is made even clearer in a later version of the Pesaḥim story, which explicitly has the Roman *hegemon* saying that even if he manages to kill all the Jews in his realm, "who will kill for us those in Babylonia and Elam and other lands"? The narrative ends with the following metaphor: "Of course, the owner [God] knows where he put his tools [the people of Israel]; when he returns to his house [the Land, or the Temple], he will restore the tools to his house." Nonetheless, Gafni continues to read these narratives and representations as "attempts to find a bright side to what is in essence a painful reality."[26] I cannot prove him wrong, surely not on a psychological level, but I can state with a certain degree of confidence that such an interpretation is hardly necessary or even suggested by the texts themselves.

This theme continues in tractate Pesaḥim: "Rabbi Ḥiyya teaches: 'What is it that is written, "God understood her way and he knew her place" (Job 28:23]: The Holy Blessed One knows Israel and that they would not be able to withstand the persecutions [גזרות] of the Romans; therefore he exiled them to Babylonia.' And Rabbi El'azar said: 'The Holy Blessed One only exiled Israel to Babylonia because it is lowland, like Sheol, as it says, "From the hands of Sheol I will redeem them, from death I will save them"' [Hos. 13:14]."

The first of these paired statements continues unequivocally the positive understanding of the "exile" to Babylon; it was in order to help (at least some of) the Jews escape from the terrible oppression of the Romans in Occupied Palestine. Rabbi El'azar's comment is, at the very least, ambivalent, comparing Babylonian exile to Sheol, another name for hell. I suspect that originally this was the statement of the Palestinian Amora (a talmudic Rabbi of the period from the third century AD until the completion of the Talmuds) Rabbi El'azar bar Pedat, referred to in the text as Rabbi El'azar and that it meant more or less exactly what it says—that even from that hellhole, God will redeem them. In this context, however, the Bavli reverses the meaning entirely and turns it into a positively tinged remark. The verse says that the redemption will be from the hands of Sheol, which is a low place. Babylonia, the plain is also a low place vis-à-vis Palestine. Rabbi El'azar is made to draw an analogy on these grounds and no other, going against the plain meaning of the verse. The redemption from Babylonia is thus simply compared to Sheol as another low-lying territory. The meaning of the statement becomes clearer when we read it with the determination of a later Babylonian authority who claimed: "The redemption comes first to the yeshiva in Babylon, for since Israel will be redeemed owing to their virtue, therefore shall the redemption come first to them; for this reason it says, 'There you shall be rescued; there the Lord will redeem you from the hand of your enemies.'" Even the Jews of Palestine will be redeemed owing to the virtue of the Babylonians.

Babylonia can even be described as the motherland of the Jews: "Rabbi Ḥanina says, 'It is because their language [Aramaic] is close to the language of Torah [and therefore good for the study thereof].' Rabbi Yoḥanan says, 'Because he sent them to the house of their mother. Its exemplum is of a man who becomes angry at his wife, to where does he send her? To the house of her mother.'... 'Ulla said, 'it was in order that they will eat dates and be busy with Torah.'"

The first speaker in this sequence remarks on the great advantage of Babylonia: their Semitic speech, which, since it is close to the Hebrew of Torah, promotes the study of Torah. (Not so incidentally, it is this linguistic fact that made it most consequent for the Babylonian Jews and not the Greek-speaking Jews of the eastern Roman Empire to "diasporize" with the Palestinian Rabbis.)[27] The most amazing of all these explanations for the choice of Babylon as the place of Jewish exile is Rabbi Yoḥanan, who turns the "exile" into Babylon into a homecoming to their motherland, the land from which Abraham is commanded to "Go forth from your land to the land that I will show you!"[28] The entire notion of "diaspora" as the act of forced dispersion from a single homeland is exploded by the Talmud at this moment (and by a Palestinian speaker—nay, the leader of the Palestinian Rabbis in his day). As Gafni points out, this statement reads almost as if it is "embracing of what is usually considered a uniquely Hellenistic idea, namely that Israel, like other ethnic groups, have a dual homeland [δευτέρα πατρίς]." Babylonia is portrayed here not only as a second homeland but as the original homeland from which they have come to Palestine. The concepts of homeland and Holy Land are thus, at least for these Rabbis, not coterminous.[29] Far from being sent into an oppressive situation, the Jews were brought to a refuge in the place where they would feel most at home—returning home, owing to their ancient roots and cultural ties with that place.[30]

There is ambivalence signified here. Even though Babylonia is pictured repeatedly as a place of refuge, there is nonetheless a sense of exile from the Holy Land that is encoded. A bride being sent to her mother's house is, of course, the sign of at least a temporary dissolution of a marriage. This does not mean that the Jews abandoned the ancient hope to be restored to the Holy Land but—as so poignantly evoked, especially by Jewish liturgy—this was an apocalyptic hope, for the end of times, for the whole world and not even a structuring principle for life in the here and now. For the nonce, despite having been exiled from the husband's house, we are at home in the mother's safe refuge and warm embrace. There is an amusing doubling of this ambiguity in the statement of ʿUlla, too, for after having praised the abundance of Babylonia and the possibility of studying Torah owing to the abundance of food in the form of dates, he remarks that he spent the better part of his first night there on the toilet and wonders how they manage to study Torah at all there! Nonetheless, asserts the Talmud: "We [in Babylonia] have made ourselves the equal of Palestine" (Gittin 6a).

One Pirkoi ben Baboi,[31] an important (if, until recently, nearly forgotten) author in eighth-century Babylonia (born, at least according to some modern scholars, in Palestine), went so far as to say:

> "Zion" is nothing but the yeshiva where they are distinguished [מצויינים] in Torah and mitzvot, for it says, "Writhe and groan, O daughter of Zion, like a woman in labor, for now you shall

> go out from the city and dwell in the open country; you shall go to Babylon. There you shall be rescued; there the Lord will redeem you from the hand of your enemies" [Mic. 4:10]. The redemption comes first to the yeshiva in Babylon, for just as Israel will be redeemed owing to their virtue, therefore shall the redemption come first to them; for this reason, it says, "There you shall be rescued; there the Lord will redeem you from the hand of your enemies." (Text apud Brodie)

This remarkable utterance (extreme and controversial even in its day, to be sure) simply replaces the Land of Israel with Babylonia *as* Zion via a pun in which *Ṣion* (Zion) is read etymologically as the place of excellence (*meṣuyyan*). Moreover, it is the Talmud that is taught and studied in the yeshivot (talmudic academies) of Babylon that confers this status on the place and on the community. It is the daughter of Zion who, according to the prophet, will go to Babylon and there shall she be rescued, there shall she be redeemed. Those Jews who stayed behind in Palestine will have to wait their turn for redemption, after the Jews of Babylonia, who are the reason for the redemption; because of their Talmud, which they have created and studied, they will be rescued and redeemed first.

The last point is the most extreme and controversial of Pirkoi's argument. The Jews of late antiquity had built Jerusalem in Babylonia's green and pleasant land; but for most, their orientation toward the old Zion was vital through all of late antiquity.[32] Indeed, the same passages of the Talmud that tell us of the synagogue that had literally slid from the Holy Land to Babylonia, bringing the Shekhina with it, also informs us that all the synagogues of Babylonia will return (this time, for sure, miraculously) to Palestine when the Messiah comes. Pirkoi's supersessionist claim, like supersession in general, is descriptively extreme, for the Babylonian Talmud would have no existence were it not for the Torah of Palestine that is embedded in it as its soil and its seed, this soil and seed having been transplanted like that legendary synagogue from the Land of Israel and planted in a new place.

On the other hand, as my late teacher Prof. H. Z. Dimitrovsky has pointed out: "It was doubtless not Pirkoi who created the ideological background of this propaganda and not he who initiated it. Echoes of this position, which Pirkoi represented in such a forceful manner, are heard clearly among the Sages of Babylonia, long before him."[33] And, one might add, very similar voices were heard from the geonim at the epicenter of Babylonian rabbinism a couple of centuries later, as in the text cited above from Saʿadyana. The Babylonian rabbinic claim to have replaced the Land of Israel, to having become a new Land of Israel, while surely not held by all, is thus very well established.

The Empire Writes Back: Dueling Talmuds

There are, however, two Talmuds: one that we call Palestinian (Hebrew: Yerushalmi, both an anachronism and an anatopism); the other the Babylonian, or Bavli. Each Talmud is diasporic with respect to the other in the sense that it is made up from materials from its own place and from the place of the others, thus both demonstrating and constructing the diaspora of which I speak. The Babylonian Talmud was, as its name implies, composed by Rabbis who lived in southern Mesopotamia in the province of Āsōristān of the Sasanian Empire.[34] The Palestinian Talmud was formed in that province (Syria Palaestina) of the Roman Empire. There is also a chronological difference: while the Palestinian Talmud was formed in the third to the late fourth centuries, the Babylonian talmudic activity went on to the sixth or even seventh. As described by Richard Kalmin: "The Bavli consists primarily of Tannaitic, Amoraic, and unattributed statements. . . . Tannaitic statements, or Baraitot, comprise the Bavli's earliest layer, dating from the first century CE until the early third century CE. Virtually all Tannaitic statements derive from Palestine, although a small number of Tannaim lived in Babylonia. Amoraic statements derive from rabbis who lived between the early third and the early sixth centuries CE in Babylonia, and between the early third and the late fourth centuries CE in Palestine."[35]

Before I go on describing the formal (or perhaps informal) literary characteristics of the Talmud, I want to pause and examine the implications of the description we've just read. Note that the earliest layer of the talmudic material shared by the two Talmuds consists of the Mishna (composed at the beginning of the third century), an entirely Palestinian work in Hebrew—the language, of course, of the Jews of Palestine.[36] It must be observed that much, if not most, of the material quoted in the name of Amoraim, whether Palestinian or Babylonian, is also in Hebrew, suggesting that the Palestinian language was the language of study, at least, in both centers, even later when different dialects of Aramaic had become the spoken tongue in both places. Palestinian and Babylonian Amoraic material is also found cheek by jowl in both Talmuds. It is, for the most part, the connective, narrative material in the Talmuds that we find in the local Aramaic dialects, Galilean and Babylonian Jewish Aramaic, respectively. In terms of linguistic formation, of their heteroglossia, then, the two great literary texts of Jewish late antiquity, the one from the East and the one from the West (according to *their* terminology: Palestine is marked geographically and not theologically in this phrase), are very closely related (although, of course, the dialectal differences in the Aramaic render each immediately recognizable to the cognoscenti). It is the interplay between the closeness and the foreignness that constitutes these two texts as diasporic with respect to each other. Each is also a diaspora with respect to itself, incorporating the signs of local and trans-local cultural context and production.

Returning to Kalmin's fine account of things, we find further literary differences between the production in the two centers:

> The Bavli contains legal pronouncements on civil, criminal, and ritual matters. It also contains sententious sayings, advice, dream interpretations, magical incantations, medical cures, polemics, folk tales, fables, legends, scriptural interpretations

> (midrash), legal case reports, and numerous other literary genres. Much more so than Palestinian rabbinic compilations, the Bavli is encyclopedic in character, meaning that it contains more varieties of rabbinic literature than roughly contemporary Palestinian compilations. The Bavli, for example, is much richer in nonlegal scriptural commentary (aggadic midrash) than is the Yerushalmi, which is more narrowly focused on law and Mishnah commentary. Apparently, the relatively narrow focus of the Yerushalmi is due in part to the fact that compilations of aggadic midrash circulated in Palestine, in contrast to the situation in Babylonia.[37]

We have, then, two Talmuds very closely related but also in competition with each other. Needless to say, the Palestinian Sages did not willingly accept the decentering of the Holy Land. There is a highly evocative text in the Palestinian Talmud (Yerushalmi) in which that resistance is made manifest. The context is of a Sage who has left Palestine, owing to the persecutions of the Romans, to set up a fully independent functioning rabbinic polity on the banks of the Pakod River in Babylonia:

> Ḥananiah the nephew of Rabbi Yehoshua intercalated [added a leap month to the year to keep the solar and lunar calendars synchronized] outside the Land. Rabbi [Yehuda Hannasi] sent him three letters with Rabbi Yitzḥak and Rabbi Natan: In the first, he wrote, "To his Holiness Rabbi Ḥananiah." In the second, he wrote, "The kids that you have left behind have become billy goats." In the third, he wrote, "If you don't accept [our authority], go out in the wilderness of the bramble, and you be the slaughterer and Neḥunion the Priest who sprinkles the blood."[38] He read the first and honored them; the second and honored them. When he read the third, he wished to discredit them. They said to him, "You cannot, as you have already honored us!" Rabbi Yitzḥak stood up and read in the

> Torah: “These are the festivals of Ḥananiah the nephew of Rabbi Yehoshua.” They said to him: “These are festivals of the Lord.” He said to them, “That’s our version.” Rabbi Natan got up and completed [that is, read the portion from the Prophets]: “For from Babylon will go out the Torah, and the Word of the Lord from Nehar Paqod!” They said, “For from Zion will go out the Torah, and the Word of the Lord from Jerusalem.” He said, “That’s our version.” (PT Nedarim 50a)[39]

This brilliant little narrative practically drips with venomous sarcasm. The Rabbi, having left Palestine during a time of Roman persecution, sets himself up to perform the duty of intercalating the calendar in Babylon, which had previously been an exclusive prerogative of the Nasi’s court in Jerusalem. Rabbi Yehuda Hannasi, hearing of this, sends along some tricky letters and tricky messengers to dissuade him from this rebellious act of setting up a new Zion. The first letter is simply a letter of praise to him, so he praises and honors the messengers in return. In the second letter, the messengers are praised by Rabbi Yehuda, who had sent them. These who were young kids when you left are now full-grown billy goats, a figure for great Talmud scholars. Of course, he praises them again.

The third letter contains the kicker—or rather, two kickers. First, he is told that if he persists in his “rebellion,” he should go out into the desert and rule over the brambles and thornbushes, and, second, he is compared to another Ḥananiah, Onias, who built a Temple in Egypt to compete with the Jerusalem one, an incredibly powerful figure of schism. At this point, Ḥananiah tries to discredit the couriers but cannot, as they have already been credited by him. These now press the attack. Sarcastically and mercilessly parodying the verse “These are the festivals of the Lord,” when one is called up to read from the Torah, he reads it: “These are the festivals of Ḥananiah.” In other words, he implies, Ḥananiah’s calendar rebels against the calendar of the Lord and replaces it with a human one. The people, not quite getting the point, reply, but the verse says, "These are the festivals of the Lord!" to which Rabbi Yitzḥak returns, Yes, that is what's written in *our* Torah, but apparently in yours (you Babylonians), it says, "The festivals of Ḥananiah." The trick is repeated when Rabbi Natan reads the portion from the Prophets and recites, "For from Babylon will go out Torah and the Word of the Lord from Nehar Paqod [the place in Babylonia where Ḥananiah was sitting]."

Once again, the people are tricked into supplying the correct reading and receive the same comeuppance. It is, of course, amazing that by the time of the great French German Rabbenu Tam (as mentioned above), the Babylonian, diasporized Torah tradition had so won the field that he could take this sarcastic parody of the verse and appropriate it, entirely unsarcastically, to mean: indeed, the Torah goes out from Bari and the Word of the Lord from Otranto. Only a few generations later (fourteenth century), both appropriating Rabbenu Tam and referring to Rabbenu Tam and his Rhineland fellow rabbis, a Sefardic Talmud scholar would declaim, "For out of Tzarefat [France] will go out the Torah, and the Word of the Lord from Ashkenaz [the Rhineland]."[40] The very diasporic adventures of the parodic saying mirror the ways that the Babylonian Talmud produces a diasporic and diasporist culture.

Needless to say, when the Babylonians tell this same story, its meanings are quite reversed.[41] In that Talmud, the story appears at Berakhot 63a–b:

> Rav Safra said: Rabbi Abbahu used to relate: When Ḥanina,[42] nephew of Rabbi Yehoshua, went into the Exile, he used to intercalate the years and determine the beginning of months outside the Land. They sent after him two Sages: Rabbi Yose the son of Kiper and the son of Zechariah the son of Kabutal. When he [Ḥanina] saw them, he said to them: Why have you come here? They said: to learn Torah we have come. He declared about them: These men are the giants of their generation, and

> their fathers served in the Temple! . . . He [Ḥanina] would declare something impure, and they declared it pure; he would say that something was permitted, and they would say forbidden. He declared of them: These men are worthless, and they are tohu! They said to him: You have already built; you may not tear down. You have already fenced in; you may not break down the fence. He said to them, What is the reason that what I declare impure, you declare pure and what I declare forbidden, you declare permitted? They said to him, because you intercalate years and determine months outside the Land. He said to them, But didn't Akiva the son of Yosef [the great Rabbi Akiva] intercalate years and determine months outside the Land? They said to him: Leave Rabbi Akiva aside, for he had not left behind him in the Land of Israel anyone as great as he was. He [Ḥanina] said: Also I have not left behind me in the Land of Israel as great as I. They said: the kids that you have left behind have become billy goats with horns, and it is they who sent us after you, and they said to us, go and say to him in our name. If he obeys, it is good, and if not, he will be excommunicated. And say to our brothers in the Exile [that they should reject Ḥanina if he does not obey them]: if they obey, it is good, and if not, they should go up to a mountain where Aḥia [their leader] will build an altar, Ḥanina will play the harp, and all will apostasize and say they have no portion in the god of Israel!
>
> All the people began to low and cry and said: God forbid; we do have a portion in the god of Israel! And why all this fuss [on the part of the Palestinians] because it says, "for from Zion will go out Torah and the word of the Lord from Jerusalem!"[43]

We can see that the story is the same but has been subtly manipulated in its transfer from the Palestinian to the Babylonian Talmud. The Palestinians still "win," but a crucial ideological difference is inscripted. The crux is in the phrase: "The kids that you have left behind have become billy goats." In the Palestinian Talmud, this is a compliment to Rabbi Ḥananiah: those young pupils whom you trained have become great Talmud scholars, which Rabbi Ḥananiah accepts as a compliment and then realizes that this means that he has approbated these very hostile emissaries. In the Babylonian Talmud's version, it means something else. Now it is a contest of where the greater Torah scholars are to be found—in Babylonia or in Palestine—and the emissaries from Palestine are made to claim that those young students whom he left behind have become great scholars and, therefore, his claim to be able to intercalate in Babylonia (as the greatest scholar in the world) is invalid. Now the ideological point is that the Palestinians are made to admit that, should it be the case that the greater talmudic scholarship is in Babylonia, then Babylonia is now the new Zion (*ṢiYYoN)*, the place where Torah study is excellent (*meṢuYYaN*), just as the Babylonian Rabbis have claimed in many of the texts that I have cited in this chapter. According to the Palestinian Talmud's version of the story, Palestine is always and forever the only Holy Land and sole center of authority: "For from Zion will go out Torah and the word of the Lord from Jerusalem"—no metaphors, no transfers, no diaspora.

The Babylonian Talmud is aware of this resistance from Palestine and seems not always sure that they are not right; there can be defensiveness in the defense. In tractate Ketubbot, the Rabbis are commenting on the verse from Ps. 87:5: "And of Zion it shall be said, this and that man was born in her: and the highest himself shall establish her." And the Rabbis comment: "Rabbi Mayesha the grandson of Rabbi Yehoshua ben Levi, 'One who waits to see her [Zion] is the same as [as good as] one who was born there.' Abbaye said 'One of them [of the Palestinian Rabbis] is as good as two of us.' Rava said, 'But one of us who goes up to there is better than two of them, for Rabbi Yermia when he was here, he had no idea what the Rabbis were saying, now that he has gone up to there, he calls us *Stupid Babylonians*' [75a]."

This little story, like many in the Talmud, captures a world of ambiguity within its multiple ironies. Rabbi Yermia, born in Babylonia but gone to Palestine to study there in the academy, was known for his cleverness, if not his politeness. When some Babylonian Torah is cited, he frequently says: "Stupid Babylonians,[44] haven't you heard that so-and-so has said?" Rava here is acknowledging the Babylonians' dependence on Palestine for traditions but asserting the superiority of the Babylonian ability to develop and understand these traditions.

At the same time, there is not a little self-deprecation in the recitation that one who waits to see Zion is as good as one who was born there (and, it should be mentioned, not a little of such self-deprecation of Babylonia versus Palestine throughout the Babylonian Talmud, as well). In his extensive and illuminating discussion of the last pages of tractate Ketubbot, Jeffrey Rubenstein has demonstrated the extent of the inner tension produced within the Babylonian academy—perhaps not coincidentally, Pumbedita, as we shall see in the next chapter—between praise of the Holy Land and a strong sense of being at home in Babylonia.[45] Perhaps, rather than soil and seed, a better metaphor might be (with apologies to Paul at Romans 9) a scion of the vines of the Land of Israel grafted onto Babylonian rootstock, or, even better, a Babylonian scion grafted onto Palestinian rootstock. That graft was constantly being renewed, and we even know how, as we will see below. Pirkoi ben Baboi has gone "too far" descriptively in his quest to establish the primacy of the Babylonian center over the Palestinian, but he has nonetheless articulated an important point: the Babylonian-ness, to which I would insist on adding the essential Palestinian-ness, of that text. It is in my view that doubled location that marks both Talmuds as diasporic texts. In the next chapter, instead of explicit declarations of such diasporicity, I hope to show how the talmudic text is discursively arranged to produce and manifest diasporicity, to construct a diasporic folk.

Chapter 3

In the Land of Talmud: The Textual Making of a Diasporic Folk

> From the eleventh century on, the Jewry of the world was not only under the regime of the talmudic halakha but in the realm of the talmudic culture. The Talmud became the book of the whole people and its songs, its daily conversation, and its discourse. Even more than the Bible, it was the Talmud that was the unifying and uniting force of the diasporas of Israel.
>
> —Hayyim Zalman Dimitrovsky[1]

In accordance with the definition of diaspora offered in Chapter 1, a diaspora is formed when two or more collectives have a doubled cultural location at home, as it were, and abroad.

Thinking about the Babylonian Talmud, we find a mixture of genres and a mixture of languages (early Hebrew, later Hebrew, Palestinian Aramaic, Babylonian Aramaic, Greek, and Persian), as well as a mixture of representations of speakers of those languages. The writers of the two Talmuds were doubly oriented, to the place where they were and to the other place where their fellow Rabbis were—in Palestine or Iranian Babylonia, respectively. It is this characteristic of doubled consciousness and doubled locale that I call "diaspora." We are a long time and far away from those Jews who sang, "By the rivers of Babylon, there we sat down, yea, we wept, when we remembered Zion. We hanged our harps upon the willows in the midst thereof. For there they that carried us away captive required of us a song; and they that wasted us required of us mirth, saying, Sing us one of the songs of Zion. How shall we sing the Lord's song in a strange land?" By late antiquity, Jews were singing the Lord's song (or rather, writing the Lord's prose) by the rivers of Babylon, and some were imagining it as a (or even *the*) new Zion. As we have observed in the previous chapter, the Babylonian center, notwithstanding a certain degree of residual self-doubt, considered itself fully the equal, and even the superior, of the Palestinian center. How did this diasporic community come into being and maintain itself as such?

The Couriers of Talmud

Cultures do not respect the limes, the borders of empires. That may well be the case; nonetheless, for my synchronic definition of diaspora to stand, there must be ways of communication between the various groups inhabiting the transnational spaces. The means by which the culture of Talmud crossed the limes is figured in the Talmud as well.

There are dozens of narratives within the Talmud about the נחותי, *naḥote*, or descenders, traveling Rabbis who went to Palestine from Babylonia and reported on what was happening in the academies there and brought back with them further news of their responses and other novellae. This activity produced a republic of traditions just as vibrant as the Republic of Letters of early modern Europe.[2]

A good illustration of the process of inter-imperial communication and composition can be found in tractate Shabbat 108b: "Rabbi Yehuda bar Ḥaviva teaches: One does not salt radishes or eggs on Sabbath. Rav Ḥizkia in the name of Abbaye says: Radish is forbidden; egg is permitted. Rav Naḥman said: I used to salt radishes, saying [that is, thinking], I actually am spoiling them, for Shmuel says that sharp radishes are superior. Since I heard the following that when ʿUlla came, he said: In the West, they salt [radishes] one piece at a time; as for salting, I don't salt, but as for dipping them [in salt], I certainly do dip them."

Rabbi Yehuda bar Ḥaviva was a Palestinian amora of the third century but a student of Shmuel, who was the rabbinic leader of Babylonian Jewry. He must, accordingly, have traveled from Palestine to Babylonia for his studies and then returned. He is cited here as teaching that one may not salt a radish or an egg on the Sabbath because this is similar to pickling or cooking it. Another (Babylonian) view is then cited that splits between the two: radishes no, eggs yes (presumably, one does not in any way pickle an egg by adding salt). Rav Naḥman then retails a bit of his autobiography, announcing that he previously followed a more lenient view and salted radishes because he was of the opinion (following his teacher, Shmuel) that salting radishes spoils them rather than pickling them, so this is not a form of cooking; but then when ʿUlla arrived from Palestine (as he is reported to have done more than eighty times in the Talmud), he reported that there, they do not salt a pile of radishes (thinking that this is like pickling) but only the individual radish that they are about to eat, and Rav Naḥman decided to follow the Palestinian practice henceforth.

Following another tradition of the same Rabbi Yehuda the son of Ḥaviva, which is irrelevant here and which I therefore skip, we encounter another traveler's tale:

> When Rav Dimi came, he said: No man has ever sunk [drowned] in the Sea of Sodom [the Dead Sea]. Rav Yosef said: Sodom is overturned, and this utterance is overturned [an allusion to the overturning of Sodom narrated in Genesis]; no man ever sank, but a board sank? [That is, why does he mention that humans don't sink there, as if other things, such as boards, do?] Abbaye said to him: He used the figure of "it is unnecessary to mention" [=לא מיבעיא, a recognized rhetorical figure in the Talmud], namely, one doesn't need to mention a board, which doesn't sink in any water in the world, but even a

> man who would sink and drown in any of the other waters of the world, in the Sea of Sodom, does not sink.

We are treated to a report brought directly from Palestine to the effect that it is impossible for humans to sink and drown in the Dead Sea. Some mock-serious interplay follows, with Rav Yosef attacking this statement as ridiculous, as it seems to imply that other things do sink in the Dead Sea, to which a standard form of rhetorical hermeneutic is applied. Naturally, the next thing the Talmud asks is:

> What difference does [knowing] this make? [It makes a difference for] this: Rabbin was walking behind Rabbi Yermia on the banks of the Sea of Sodom. [Rabbin] said: may we wash with these waters of the Sabbath? [That is, is it considered washing, which is permitted, or healing, which is forbidden on the Sabbath?] He [Rabbi Yermia] said: It's just fine.
>
> [Rabbin then asked:] And what about closing and opening [one's eyes, when washing in the Dead Sea on Sabbath]? Rabbi Yermia answered: That I haven't heard, but I've heard a similar case, for R. Ze'ira said, at times in R. Mattenah's name, at others in Mar 'Ukba's name, and both [R. Mattenah and Mar 'Ukba] had said it in the names of Shmuel's father and Levi: One of them [Shmuel's father or Levi] says: wine *into* the eyes is forbidden; *on* the eyes is permitted. And one said that saliva that is unmixed with food, even on the eyes, is forbidden [and we do not know who said which].[3]

So to answer our question of why it was important to know that no one ever drowns in the Dead Sea, we cite another Palestinian mini-narrative, a story in which two Rabbis are walking by the banks of that body of water, and the younger asks the older whether it is permitted to wash in the waters of the Dead Sea on the Sabbath, as we consider these waters healing for the eyes, and healing is forbidden. The implication is, of course, that we would only understand this passage if we know just how salty the Dead Sea is, and we can only know that by virtue of the statement that no human being ever sinks in those waters. The answer comes quickly that this is permitted. This is because the prohibition on healing on the Sabbath is a rabbinic one and not derived from the written Torah. The purpose of this prohibition is to prevent folks from thinking that they may crush and make medicines on the Sabbath, which is forbidden, except in the case where life might be saved. Since people just see him swimming in the water, they would not imagine that he is doing this for healing and would not be confused and go out and make drugs.

At this point, yet another question is brought up: When one is in the water of the Dead Sea on the Sabbath, may one close and open one's eyes, thus making more saltwater go in and heal them? Rav Yermia answers that he has no tradition as to this point but does have an analogy that might help: the fact that Shmuel's father and Levi have prohibited such actions where the onlooker can determine that it is for healing, and thus in our case, where onlookers would perceive one quickly opening and closing one's eyes, they might well realize that this is for healing and thus it would be forbidden.

I would like to renarrate the sugya, paying close attention to the provenience of the figures involved. We begin with the statement of Rabbi Yehuda bar Ḥaviva, a Palestinian authority, commented upon immediately by Rabbi Ḥizkia in the name of Abbaye, a well-known Babylonian authority. This Rabbi Ḥizkia has an interesting pedigree. Having been born and studied in Palestine and having continued his teaching there in the Holy Land, we find him, nonetheless, quoting (at least twice) major Babylonian authorities, as here. We have, then, a Palestinian statement, commented on by a Palestinian authority but in the name of a Babylonian one and in the Babylonian Talmud. In the next act of our little drama, we find the quintessential Babylonian, Rav Naḥman, remarking on his change of practice after getting a report about what they do in the West brought by that most assiduous of travelers from Palestine to Babylonia, ʿUlla.

From there, we move to another tradition brought to Babylonia from Palestine by a well-known traveler, Rav Dimi: the piece of information about drownings in the Dead Sea, responded to by Rav Yosef and Abbaye, two more "pure" Babylonian authorities (this is the same Abbaye cited above by the Palestinian Rabbi Ḥizkia). When the question is raised as to what difference this piece of information makes, the answer comes in a story about Rabbin, who, as we shall see later in this chapter, is another of the travelers who brought traditions from Palestine to Babylonia and back. Finally, Rabbin's question in Palestine is answered by the Palestinian Rabbi Yermia (of Babylonian origin but the teacher of said Rabbi Ḥizkia), with reference to a tradition about two very early Babylonian authorities, Shmuel's father and Levi (one trained in Palestine, one not). Whether this narrative is a true account of actual transmissions and retransmissions, it is certainly a representation of a dense web of transnational—or better, trans-imperial—oral textual connections. Given the way that each Talmud, or each community, is thus embedded in its own milieu (much Greek in Jewish Palestine; Iranian in Jewish Babylonia) while also sharing intensely and intimately in the ongoing production of a textual culture distant from them, we have a figure here for the imagining of diaspora that is quite similar, mutatis mutandis, in its structure to the black internationalism of the first half of the twentieth century, explored so richly by Brent Hayes Edwards.[4]

Narratives such as these dramatically confirm the point I made in Chapter 1: that living lateral cultural connections between diasporic communities are not marginal or exclusively a product of the Internet era, as many theoreticians of diaspora would have it, but both ancient and crucial to the constitution of diasporic cultures tout court. We can get more of a feel for these relations and their complexities by looking at another somewhat complicated story; the halakhic subject is arcane (and perhaps distasteful to some), but the rhetoric is lively and telling. The case has to do with a slaughtered animal from which a tiny piece of skin with some flesh has adhered and been touched by someone. The question is the transfer of impurity to that person. The Mishna says,

"Skin that has on it an olive's worth of flesh: one who touches a fiber of it or a hair that is on the other side of it is rendered impure." The situation is one in which the animal is impure, having been touched by an impure object such as a dead insect but still edible from the point of view of the kosher rules.[5] If a pure person touches a piece of the skin that is still attached to some of the flesh, that person becomes impure as well (and cannot, therefore, serve in the Temple). On this, the Talmud (Ḥullin 124a) comments:

> ʿUlla [Palestinian traveler] said that Rabbi Yoḥanan [Palestinian] said: This Mishna was only taught in the case where this bit came off the animal, but if it came off the knife [when the animal was being flayed], it is insignificant [and does not render the person impure]. Rav Naḥman [dominant Babylonian authority] to ʿUlla: Did Rabbi Yoḥanan include even [a piece] the size of a pan of scales [in being insignificant]?[6] He [ʿUlla] said to him [Naḥman]: Yes. And even the size of a sieve, he said to him? Yes. He [Naḥman] said to him [ʿUlla]: By G-d, even if I heard this directly from the mouth of Rabbi Yoḥanan, I would not listen to him!

There are circumstances in which touching a bit of an animal's flesh that has become impure conveys impurity. The Mishna records one such incidence, in which there is an "olive's worth," that is, the minimum significant amount throughout the Talmud, and lets us know that if someone touches that minimum amount, he or she contracts impurity. The Talmud reports that ʿUlla, whom we have just met above as one of the travelers, reported when he came to Babylonia that Rabbi Yoḥanan, the greatest leader of Palestinian Jewry, had restricted the impact of this ruling by confining it to the situation in which this olive's worth of flesh had come off the animal itself, but when it had merely flown off the knife, according to Rabbi Yoḥanan, it was considered insignificant and, therefore, did not convey impurity. Rav Naḥman is, to say the least, astounded, since it seems that Rabbi Yoḥanan is implying (or openly stating) that any size of flesh that flies off the knife is insignificant. He inquires of the talmudic plenipotentiary if this is the case and is assured that it is. On this, Rav Naḥman remarks that even if he heard this from Rabbi Yoḥanan himself, he would not have accepted it.

In the next act of the story, the report of Rav Naḥman's response travels back to Palestine: "When Rabbi ʿOshaya went up [to Palestine from Babylonia], he found Rabbi ʿAmmi [born in Babylonia but resident in Tiberias as one of Rabbi Yoḥanan's principal disciples] and told him this tradition: 'This is what ʿUlla said, and this is what Rav Naḥman answered him.' He [ʿAmmi] said to him [ʿOshaya], 'and because Rav Naḥman is the son-in-law of the House of the Patriarch [בי נשיאה], he so disdains the utterances of Rabbi Yoḥanan?'"

As we will see below, Rav Naḥman is repeatedly accused of arrogance, owing to his connection with the *Reish Galuta*, the temporal head of Babylonian Jewry, who claimed equal status with the Nasi, his counterpart in Palestine. His statement that even had he heard it from the great Palestinian himself, he would not have accepted it, is taken as such insolence, but the story is not yet over:

> After a time, he [ʿOshaya] found him [ʿAmmi] sitting [teaching] and reporting this utterance [of Rabbi Yoḥanan's] about the second clause in the Mishna: "If it had on it two half-olives' worth, they cause impurity when carried but not when touched, the words of Rabbi Ishmael; Rabbi Akiva says neither when touched or carried. This Mishna was only taught in the case where this bit came off the animal, but if it came off from the knife, it is insignificant [and does not render the person impure]."
>
> He [ʿOshaya] said to him, "Does the Master [that is, you, ʿAmmi] teach [Rabbi Yoḥanan's statement] about the second clause?" He said to him, "Yes, and did ʿUlla teach it to you about the first clause?" He [ʿOshaya] said to him, "Yes." He

> [ʿAmmi] said to him: "By G-d, if it had been said to me by Joshua the son of Nun, I would not have listened to it."

The Mishna didn't only have one clause. In the second clause, we find a controversy between two major tannaim (early Rabbis) about a situation in which two half-olives' worth of flesh are attached to the skin, and the question is whether the two separate pieces add up to one olive's worth. In this context, the restriction of Rabbi Yoḥanan makes perfect sense, for now the size is already given as tiny. If the small bit came off the animal, it conveys impurity because it was attached to the whole animal; but if it comes off the knife, it was already detached and thus insignificant. Even Rabbi ʿAmmi, Rabbi Yoḥanan's loyal student and defender, understands Rav Naḥman's pugnacious response. Rabbi ʿAmmi confesses that, had he heard this (ostensibly) erroneous tradition, he would have reacted exactly as Rav Naḥman did, and even if he heard it from the second-greatest prophet of all time, Joshua. So, it would seem, peace was restored to the Diaspora. Rav Naḥman, leader of the Babylonians, and Rabbi Yoḥanan, leader of Palestinians, were restored to mutual respect and harmony. But there is another surprise for the reader: "When Rabbin and all the travelers came, they said it about the first clause!" (Ḥullin 124a).[7]

We have already met Rabbin as one of the traveling bearers of Palestinian Talmud to Babylonia, and here we meet him again. Contradicting the narrative of Rabbis ʿOshaya and ʿAmmi, it seems that ʿUlla's original report was accurate and thus that Rav Naḥman's arrogant attack on Rabbi Yoḥanan might have been justified. The matter is left unresolved.

The discursive entangling of the Palestinian and Babylonian authorities is rich and revealing. Let me recapitulate with a few fewer details. ʿUlla, a late third-century Palestinian Rabbi known for making frequent trips between the Palestinian and Babylonian communities, reports a comment on a clause of the Mishna in the name of the great Palestinian leader, Rabbi Yoḥanan, to the dominant figure in Babylonian rabbinism of his day, Rav Naḥman. Rav Naḥman finds this statement as reported by 'Ulla incredible and remarks, somewhat aggressively, that, had he heard it directly from the mouth of the master himself, he would not have believed or accepted it. 'Ulla goes back to Palestine and relates *this* story to Rabbi 'Ammi, a disciple of Rabbi Yoḥanan, who protests that Rav Naḥman's disdainful tone with respect to Rabbi Yoḥanan can only be explained by Rav Naḥman, the *Babylonian*, having especially close ties with the family of the patriarch, the government-recognized head of Babylonian Jewry, usually referred to as ריש גלותא, head of the Exile. This is an interesting comment in that it marks Rav Naḥman, though an important rabbinic leader, as being separately emplaced from the point of view of class such that he can be disrespectful to the greatest Palestinian Rabbi of his day.[8]

We then discover that 'Ulla has seemingly misreported what it was that Rabbi Yoḥanan had said, thus (misleadingly and unintentionally) fomenting Rav Naḥman's contempt. Rabbi Yoḥanan had not made his statement—says 'Ammi—with respect to that clause of the Mishna that so startled Rav Naḥman but with respect to another clause, where it is much more plausible. Indeed, adds Rabbi 'Ammi, had I heard the story as 'Ulla had told it, I myself (Rabbi 'Ammi) would not have accepted it, not only from Rabbi Yoḥanan but even from Joshua bin Nun himself.[9] It would seem that it all had a happy ending—a miscommunication easily resolved.

But another surprise awaits us: it transpires that *all* the travelers, those professional transferrers of learning from Palestine to Babylonia and, as we've seen, back again, report that Rabbi Yoḥanan said what he said as 'Ulla had originally reported it—that he had made the statement that would apparently justify Rav Naḥman's contempt. In either case, what we see is the representation of a community of learners sending traditions back and forth from the Sasanian to the Roman territories and engaging each other actively and mutually. We have a tradition of lively intercourse between the Babylonian and Palestinian centers. It would not be entirely accurate to say that the Babylonian Talmud takes

Palestinian traditions and works on them, given the back-and-forth, the mutual exchange, critique, and comment, represented in this narrative and many other such narratives.

I am not claiming that this and other parallel stories really happened in the way that they are recounted but rather that they represent at least the Babylonian understanding of their diasporic condition in ways that match the descriptions of such conditions as given above. The Babylonian center is independent enough for its leader to be able to state that he would reject the sayings of the leader of the Palestinian center. Note how the term בי נשיאה, house of the patriarch, usually reserved for the Roman-appointed head of the Jews in Palestine, has been appropriated for the ריש גלותא, "head of the Exile," the political leader of Babylonian Jewry, establishing a kind of parity (in the construction of this text) between the two Jewries, each thus diasporic with respect to the other. Both "houses of the patriarch" are said to have been descended directly from King David. The two places share back-and-forth traditions and comments on an almost equal footing; it is the shared enterprise of interpreting the Mishna that constitutes them as a collective.

It is this type of collective, analogous to Paul Gilroy's Black Atlantic, for instance,[10] that I would figure as being worth isolating and theorizing under the sign of diaspora, giving that term a meaning specific enough to be diagnostic and general enough to be useful as a taxon. In this way, the Jewish diasporas can be dispersed and recovered in an entirely new key, as a complex and nuanced set of examples for the historical and theoretical investigation of diaspora as a phenomenon or a way of construing certain historical human practices. My argument is that older views that read the Jewish diaspora as unique (or nearly so) and determinative for the definition of diaspora are wrong and, on the other hand, the innovative thoughts about diaspora emerging from the theoretical literature do not support the view (held by some such theoreticians) that "the" Jewish diaspora—ironically—is exceptional in the history of diasporas.[11] In contrast, I assert that the new approaches can be supported and deepened from analysis of Jewish diaspora, or set of diasporas. In the next section, we will observe how these same Babylonian talmudists are also deeply located within their own Babylonian/Iranian context, Jewish and non-Jewish; it is that doubled consciousness—the souls of Jew-folk—that produces the diasporic cultural condition.

The Iranian Talmud

No one can seriously doubt any more that the Babylonian Talmud is much embedded within an Iranian cultural context.[12] In a series of publications, Yaakov Elman, his students, and other scholars have begun to explore in depth and breadth aspects of the Talmud's law and lore that are clearly part and parcel of its cultural location in Iran.[13] In particular, the work of Shai Secunda, one of Elman's most distinguished young protégés, has greatly enriched our understanding.[14] My task will be to attempt to integrate their results into a broader descriptive account of the synchronic state of Babylonian rabbinic culture and the Babylonian Talmud, in accordance with my view that diaspora is a synchronic state of doubled (or more) cultural location.

The definition I have proposed for diaspora in general and undertaken to illustrate via analysis of the Babylonian Talmud involves a double location of culture, an orientation in which a collective is both in its cultural location and also somewhere else at the same time, thus both inside and outside a local culture. This condition is usually described as obtaining within the modern situation of the Jews or as part of a postcolonial, racialized, or sexualized situation of particular groups of people, thus, the mimic men of Bhabha, the doubled consciousness of the souls of black folk of Du Bois,[15] the *gaie savoir* of Halperin. My purpose here is to understand this situation of doubled cultural location as the prime, and even defining, moment for the Jewish diaspora(s), at least as far back as late antiquity. In contrast, once again, to the commonplace reading of this situation as a situation of more or less acute discomfort,

I read it as the source of the particular kind of creativity that empowers Jews and other diasporic peoples.[16] I emphasize again that this is not a matter of right or wrong interpretation but of focusing different lenses or filters on the same material.

An example: while Isaiah Gafni emphasizes the eagerness to come to Palestine exhibited by the Babylonian Rabbi Zeʿira, noting in passing the objections of his teacher to that move,[17] I would emphasize more the statement of that teacher, Rav Yehuda, who actually declares it forbidden by the Torah to leave Babylonia (Shabbat 41a); poor Zeʿira has to trick his teacher and sneak out for the Holy Land like a thief in the night. This background certainly tempers or ironizes Rabbi Zeʿira's zeal, rendering it near comic. In making that statement, Rav Yehuda is insisting that Babylonia has the same status as Palestine. Just as, according to many Rabbis, it is forbidden to leave the latter, it is forbidden to leave the former: "Rav Yehuda said: Anyone who goes up from Babylonia to Palestine violates a positive commandment of the Torah, for it says, 'To Babylonia they will be brought, and there they shall remain, until I remember them, the utterance of the Lord'" (Jer. 27:22, Ketubbot 110b). Gafni's attempt to make this and similar statements a response to the increasing emphasis of the Palestinians that delegitimate the Diaspora remains a hypothesis and a possibility but certainly cannot be taken as a necessary conclusion.[18] If the ideological roots of "Zionism" are to be found in Palestinian traditions of the amoraic period, as Gafni himself lightly suggests, so the roots of diasporism, or even anti-Zionism, can be found within the Talmud, as acknowledged, too, by Gafni.[19]

The very (perhaps bitter) dialogue between Palestinian and Babylonian versions of a narrative, one Talmud prohibiting a certain Jew from going from Palestine even to perform the mitzvah of honoring their dead while the other Talmud prohibits a certain Jew from leaving Babylonia for Khuzistan to perform the mitzvah of levirate marriage, is, in my view, exactly what constitutes these two communities and texts as in diasporic relations with each other.[20] The only way that these dueling versions of the story could possibly come into existence is via the ongoing vital cultural, linguistic, and textual connections between the two communities, the two texts. Ironically, one of the strongest pieces of evidence that Gafni has for Palestinian disdain for Babylonian immigrants and denunciation of the Babylonian Jews is found in the Babylonian Talmud.[21] The examples could be multiplied.

The question, for me, is not to what extent the Babylonian (or, for that matter, the Palestinian) Rabbis extolled the Land of Israel but what kind of actual cultural and social relations obtained between Jewish collectives in late antiquity as construed or constructed by the texts. We have seen above that the Palestinian Talmud is as full of citations and discussions of Babylonian Rabbis as the Babylonian Talmud is full of Palestinians.[22] Once again, Gafni, with his extraordinary acumen, puts his finger on this distinction (without quite phrasing it as I have). Of a story told in a late tannaitic text of three Rabbis going abroad and breaking down and weeping at the border, Gafni remarks: "All this weeping notwithstanding, of the rabbis mentioned in the story Judah b. Bathyra became a prominent rabbinic authority in Nisibis, Matya b. Heresh assumed an important position in Rome, and Ḥananiah, nephew of R. Joshua, scandalized the rabbinic community by attempting to intercalate the calendar in Babylonia."[23] Of these, it must be said that the last, already mentioned above, is most telling for my thesis, since the intercalation of the month is always done on the basis of meteorological phenomena observed in Palestine; so by his act, this Ḥananiah would be asserting the equal status of Babylonia. The same Ḥananiah who allegedly wept at leaving the Holy Land nonetheless finds himself in strong conflict only a few years later with the leaders of that same Holy Land rabbinic community, owing to his assertion of the independence, and even primacy, of the Babylonian center. The strong import of the narratives of these Rabbis' fates in life is not whether they cried on leaving the Land but how they, rather like our four captive medieval Rabbis from Chapter 1, became founders and leaders in very important centers of Jewish learning.

These complex relations between the two centers are frequently commented on in the Talmud via anecdotes (as is so much of what it has to say). In an extensive study of a passage of the Babylonian Talmud dealing with customs having to do with banqueting, Gafni student Geoffrey Herman demonstrates that the signal for ending a meal in Palestine was the drinking of a final glass of wine and the grace after meals; in Babylonia, it was a second washing of the hands before the grace and the removal of the individual tray table. In his elaborate discussion, Herman shows that the Babylonian Talmud revises Palestinian sources to fit Persian, Sasanian customs that are also their own. The halakhic demonstration is too long and complex to sum up here, but a little anecdote that the Bavli cites (produces), according to Herman, thematizes this difference in a nearly comic and culturally ironic fashion: "Rav and Rabbi Ḥiyya were sitting at a meal in front of Rabbi [Yehuda Hanasi]. Rabbi said to Rav, 'Get up and wash your hands!' He [Rabbi Ḥiyya] saw that he [Rav] was trembling. He said to him: 'Worthless one! He was saying to you, "prepare yourself to lead us in the grace after meals."'"[24]

Rav was a new immigrant to Palestine—who later returned to Babylonia and became the dominant force in the institution of rabbinic Judaism there—and to the house of its leader, Rabbi. When Rabbi ordered him to get up and wash his hands, he took this as a sign of disfavor, implying that his hands were dirty. His predecessor from Babylonia among the Palestinian worthies explained to him that it was the opposite; Rabbi wanted to honor him with leading the company in the grace. The cultural irony in the story is that the Bavli, when it tells it, makes the Babylonian custom and not the Palestinian one the center of the story, for it is, as Herman has shown, there in the Sasanian realms—not in Palestine—that the meal ended with a ritual washing of hands.[25] Aware of the difference between Babylonian and Palestinian customs and even when thematizing it in the story, the Bavli nonetheless inverts the relations and supplies a Sasanian custom, a second hand washing at the end of the meal, instead of a Roman one for the upper-class Palestinian, Rabbi—presumably, so that the Babylonian audience will understand what is going on. Clearly, the prime cultural reference world for the Babylonian storyteller is Sasanian Babylonia.

After such work on the part of Elman and his students (especially Shai Secunda),[26] Gafni and his students, and others who have joined the endeavor, the Iranian cultural context of the Bavli may not be gainsaid.

Doubling Culture

We must not let the excitement of what we are learning from this scholarship lead (paradoxically) to a less than full and nuanced account of what counts as context for the Babylonian Talmud. If we return to the story just told, we can see further dimensions in the play of the two cultures. As Tal Hever-Chybowski has remarked, the point of using the Sasanian custom for the setting of the confusion in Palestine is not merely to make the story legible to its Babylonian audience but also to make it funny for them. As he points out: "This joke is precisely diasporic because it relies on the doubled cultural knowledge. The comic inversion of custom only emphasizes the duality, the in-betweenness, the fact that the intercultural contact here is not one-directional but rather doubled. The direction is blurred; it's not a Babylonian custom translated to a Palestinian one or vice versa—it's an absurd, circular, illogical confusion between the locales, without a center or a periphery."[27] The play of the two sets of customs and the comic inversions that result from this play speak not only of an Iranian/Sasanian context for the Babylonian Talmud but of a double-centered or decentered one, one of diaspora. This can be borne out by looking at halakhic material in the Talmud as well.

A case in point is an argument by Richard Kalmin, who proposes that "Persian attitudes and practices with regard to idols and idol worship also had a significant impact on Babylonia, constituting another respect in which Babylonia was more Persian than Roman during the period under discussion."[28] Kalmin's own data belie this conclusion and suggest something far more interesting: the dual cultural orientation of the Babylonian Rabbis and the Babylonian Talmud for which I am arguing. Kalmin cites many examples within the Babylonian Talmud of

Palestinian Rabbis confronting idols and idol worship but virtually none with respect to Babylonian Rabbis. Arguing for a basis in historical reality for this difference, Kalmin suggests that this is a good fit for the current scholarly conclusion of vast differences with respect to the worship of statues between the Roman Empire and Sasanid Persia in which such worship was taboo:

> Turning to rabbinic attitudes toward idols in the rabbinic present, we obtain what appears to be a markedly different result. Given the paucity of evidence for the existence of idols in Sasanian Babylonia, we would expect Babylonian rabbis to view the temptation to worship idols as a thing of the distant past, all but irresistible to biblical Israelites, but whose day has passed, such that in the rabbinic present it was only necessary to deal with idolatry, if at all, in its guise as a gentile practice. Contrary to what we would expect, however, the Bavli provides a record of late antique rabbinic anxiety about idolatry, which would appear at first glance to lead to the conclusion that it remained a potent force in Sasanian Babylonia.[29]

After compellingly showing us that an extended text in the Babylonian Talmud Avoda Zara 54b–55a demonstrates significant rabbinic anxiety about the attractions of and arguments for idolatry in the Babylonian milieu,[30] Kalmin concludes:

> Babylonian rabbis, therefore, viewed idol worship as a significant threat, and arguments in its favor provoked rabbinic anxiety and demanded refutation. Even though my survey of literary evidence for direct Babylonian rabbinic contact with idols turned up very little, the above discussion suggests that this evidence does not tell the whole story. Dramatic stories depicting the power of idols circulated in Babylonia, some deriving from Babylonia itself but others deriving from the

> Greco-Roman world or from times and places in the Persian Empire unaffected by the Sasanian destruction of idols, fueled in all likelihood by the Bible's profound obsession with idolatry, and by the tendency of any group to exaggerate the menace posed by outsiders.[31]

On the basis of these data, Kalmin comes to a remarkable judgment: "Given the evidence surveyed above, however, which indicates the paucity of idols in Persia in general and Babylonia in particular, it appears that at least in Babylonia, this continued vitality *was more in the minds of the rabbis than grounded in the realities of life in Sasanian Persia*."[32] This interpretation misses the point that the realities of life for these Babylonian Rabbis incorporated fully the reality of Roman Palestine as well. The diasporic model answers to these textual facts much better—to wit, that the anxieties of Palestine were an integral part of the everyday cultural location of the Babylonian Rabbis as well—not "in their minds" in the sense of paranoiac fantasy—a situation best conveyed by the model of diaspora that I have proffered so far. It is wrong to conclude that "Babylonia was more Persian than Roman during the period under discussion," or rather, Āsōristān may well have been more Persian than Roman, but Jewish Bavel is doubly located in Iranian Āsōristān and in Palestine at the same time.

My own conclusion is nearly opposite to Kalmin's: Rabbinic Babylonia reflects well the realia of the Sasanid Iran in which they were dwelling, but the culture that they produce is dually located, in local Iran and in trans-local Roman Palestine at the same time.[33] In place of Kalmin's "puzzling disconnect between reality 'on the ground' in Sasanian Babylonia and the rabbis' experience of the world,"[34] I would simply offer that both the ground and the world for the Babylonian Rabbis was bigger than Āsōristān and doubled, fitting my suggested parameters for the description of a diasporic culture.[35]

An impressive bit of evidence for this judgment is the fact that, as Shaul Shaked has shown, comparison of Babylonian magic bowls, the quintessential non-talmudic (non-rabbinic?) Jewish cultural product of late antiquity, to Palestinian magical amulets, shows that the latter have to be understood as the dominant cultural context of the former and not the reverse.[36] In other words, there were vectors of Jewish cultural flow from Palestine to Babylonia even outside the rabbinic routes of the *naḥote*—presumably, trade routes—and once it comes to this, likely the same trade routes that those rabbinic traveling salesmen followed. Surely, we have underestimated the impact of Iranian culture on the Jews of Babylon, but we must surely not lessen our emphasis on the connections with the West.[37] The solution is a richer understanding of the diasporic nature of the texts and cultures involved. Instead of figuring Jewish Babylonia as somewhere "between" Persia and Roman Palestine and somehow subject to influence from both sides, as Kalmin does, let us imagine it as a space of doubled and more cultural production in which immediate locale and trans-local reality are equally present and productive. As Finbarr Flood has pointed out, "*transculturation* has gained currency as a term that emphasizes the multidirectional nature of exchange."[38] The Bavli is, I suggest, in Persia and Roman Palestine, not between them. It is itself a diaspora, a transcultural space, although, to be sure, the space of Babylonia itself was also a meeting point and point of conversation between Greco-Roman and Iranian cultures.

Crossing Borders: On the Treasury of Souls

Late ancient Babylonian Jewry, thus, were at a meeting point of empires and cultures from the West and the East. The most powerful of those cultural connections to the West was to the Jews of Greco-Roman Palestine, their scholars and traditions, constituting the primary diasporic connection and, indeed, constituting this as a diaspora. But this primary connection hardly exhausts the Talmud's cultural world, as that world did not consist only of other Jews and Zoroastrians; there were Syriac-speaking Christians in that world as well (not to mention, for the moment, Helleno-Roman traditionalists). One great advantage of the diasporic model for reading the Talmud that I am developing in this book is the possibility that it affords for less dichotomous, more nuanced, interpretations of cultural connections in various directions. We need not decide whether the Babylonian Talmud is more or less Iranian than Roman, Greek than Aramaic; it is all these things, as a heteroglossic diasporic text, a text that incorporates, as we have seen above, multiple languages (in both the literal and more expansive metaphoric sense) within its capacious and porous textual, cultural borders. According to Shaul Shaked, the best explanation for the extensive Iranian cultural material to be found in Second Temple Palestinian Jewish literature is the interchange between the Jews of Persia and Mesopotamia and the Jews of Palestine during the Achaemenid period, owing to commercial and other ties between the two groups of Jews. Gafni further remarks: "Just as certain Persian concepts and attitudes might have been introduced into Palestinian Jewish society through the mediation of Jews traveling from Iran to western lands, we may note in rabbinic times a reverse phenomenon: the rabbis of Babylonia were almost certainly the recipients of certain religious and social attitudes that were spawned in a decidedly Hellenist-Roman and ultimately Christian environment."[39]

The geographical center of authority for the Babylonian Jews is in Maḥoza (Syriac, Maḥoze; a section of Seleucia-Ctesiphon, the Sasanian capital), the site of the Catholicos of the East Syrian church. As Adam Becker noted: "Jews and Christians in Mesopotamia spoke the same language, lived under the same rulers, practiced the same magic, engaged in mystical and eschatological speculation, and shared scriptures as well as a similar fixation on the ongoing and eternal relevance of those scriptures. They developed similar institutions aimed at inculcating an identity in young males that defined each of them as essentially a homo discens, a learning human, or rather, a res discens, a learning entity, since learning was understood as an essential characteristic of their humanity."[40] Given these considerations, Becker adumbrates—but in concert with the scope of his project does not develop the particulars of—the importance of this shared culture for the formation and content of the Babylonian Talmud. Whatever the lines and modes of contact between Aramaic and Greek, between Jews in the Sasanian realms and Christians in Cappadocia, there is at least one piece of evidence for the product of such contact that I take as conclusive.

In his excellent monograph on Eunomius, a late fourth-century "neo-Arian" theologian, Richard Vaggione discusses an important point of theological resonance for his hero, having to do with the nature of human souls, a point that has powerful implications for any theology of the Incarnation. The eponymous hero of Vaggione's book holds what appears to be a very strange and ostensibly unique doctrine. All human souls were created at the time of the first creation of humanity, when Adam came into being. There are, accordingly, a preestablished and finite number of souls. The condition for the end of the world is that all the pre-created souls will have lived a life in bodies.[41] Fascinatingly, the "paradigm" of the creative act by which God created the souls is the infusion of breath into Adam's body. So far, Vaggione's interpretation.[42] Piecing the doctrine together from the various sources cited by Vaggione,[43] I would take the analysis (synthesis) a bit further. A hostile witness to the Eunomian doctrine, Nemesius of Emesa, presents its foundation in the following manner: "Eunomius, then, defined the soul as a bodiless essence created in a body [agreeing with Plato and Aristotle]. For, on the one hand, the 'bodiless essence' came from the 'truth' [Plato]; on the other hand, the 'created in a body' is learned from Aristotle. He did not see, despite being clever, that what he was trying to bring together was incompatible."[44]

Vaggione remarks that "there is no need to try to 'unpack' Nemesius's criticism here or go into the background of the doctrine." For my purposes, at least a partial unpacking and going into is what is needed, for Eunomius's doctrine is fully explicable and Nemesius's objection answerable when comparison is made to an important rabbinic holding. Moreover, as we shall see, the talmudic saying is illuminated by the comparison to Eunomius as well.

At four places in the Babylonian Talmud (Yevamot 62a and 63b; Avoda Zara 5a; Nidda 13b)—and only in the Babylonian Talmud—we find the following puzzling statement: Rabbi Assi said, "The son of David will not come until all the souls in the body are finished, as it says, 'For I will not contend forever, neither will I be always wroth: for the spirit shall fail before me and the souls that I have made'" (Isa. 57:16). Rabbi Assi's midrash reads the verse to mean only when the spirit and the souls that God has made run out, as it were, before him, will the Messiah come. When the spirit and the souls "fail before me," when they are gone and finished, then, says Rabbi Assi, God will not contend or be wroth, for the redemption will have come. In other words, we find here in a midrashic word the entire content of Eunomius's controversial doctrine that there is a finite number of human souls from the beginning and that the redemption will come only when all of them have been born into bodies. This is not to deny Vaggione's elaborate reconstruction of the philosophical theology underlying Eunomius's position but to elaborate its homelier sources in traditional biblical interpretation common to some Jews and Christians. Although some antecedents to part of this doctrine—namely, the theological claim that all the pre-created souls need to be used up before the redemption can be found in the apocalyptic literature—the late ancient forms of the tradition share details not found before.[45]

I find it entirely plausible to imagine this doctrine (rather rare in the Talmud itself, as we have seen) circulating between and among Babylonian Jews and Cappadocian Christians in the fourth century. (Lest the connection seem too far-fetched, the Talmud knows of many connections between its rabbinic heroes and Cappadocia; according to Babylonian legend, none less than Rabbis Akiva and Me'ir found themselves in Cappadocia on occasion.) No wonder, then, that one Christian author, so-called pseudo-Athanasius, regards some elements of this doctrine as *secundum fabulatores Judaeos*, and, pace Vaggione, these *fabulatores* would hardly be Philo, who would never be referred to in such dismissive terms by patristic writers.[46]

There is further evidence for a rabbinic provenience for this theological idea cum interpretation, pointed out by Vaggione but, in my opinion, not fully appreciated by him. In the Clementine *Recognitions* 3.26, we find the doctrine as well: "And on this account, the world required long periods, until the number of souls that were predestined to fill it should be completed, and then that visible heaven should be folded up like a scroll, and that which is higher should appear, and the souls of the blessed, being restored to their bodies, should be ushered into light."[47] Vaggione implies that this is, perhaps, an Anomoean [Arian] interpolation in the pseudo-Clementine text, remarking that this is "a work with at least one substantial Anomoean interpolation."[48] When we consider the well-established connections between the authors of the pseudo-Clementina and Jews,[49] and even rabbinic Jews, a much more attractive hypothesis emerges through which the *Recognitions* may have been the source for Eunomius, rather than the opposite, or that the *Recognitions* provide precious evidence for the circulation of this idea, *secundum fabulatores Judaeos* (following Jewish fabulators) in fourth-century Christian circles. Further support for this point may be adduced from the image of the heavens folded like a scroll, one that appears prominently in rabbinic texts as well. The fact that the putatively "orthodox" writer of the pseudo-Athanasian text also knows that the tradition and its provenience are Jewish suggests that knowledge of this doctrine was widespread in early Christian circles.

While I thus agree with pseudo-Athanasius, on fairly plausible chronological grounds, that it is not unlikely that this doctrine has come to Eunomius following Jewish aggadists (*fabulatores*), Eunomius, in turn, helps us unravel a puzzle in the rabbinic text as well. While the medieval Jewish commentators (chiefly Rashi, in eleventh-century France) certainly understand that "in the body" is a reference to a mystical doctrine of a treasury of souls, they seem unable to explain why it is called "in the body." The scholar of rabbinic ideas E. E. Urbach held that the "body" here referred to the individual bodies into which the souls would be born,[50] an opinion rightly rejected by Sysling out of hand.[51] Sysling, however, is no more able to explain the use of the term "body" here than is Rashi himself. Eunomius's connection between this doctrine and the breathing of God's spirit into Adam solves this exegetical conundrum nicely. The "body" here is the body of the supernal Adam, and what was breathed into that body was all the souls that would ever exist, all created at that moment, as Eunomius would have it. Perhaps it is not going too far to suggest that Nemesius has (willfully?) misread Eunomius and that Eunomius's reference to the soul as being "created in a body" (ἐν σώματι κτιζομένην) should be read rather "in the body," referring to the Adamic body as well; there is no self-contradiction between "the truth" and Aristotelianism in Eunomius, either. The remarkable thing is that we have compelling evidence of cultural and religious connection of a deep, specific, and recognized sort between the Christian world of fifth-century Cappadocia and the Babylonian rabbinic world to the east and south and over the limes of the Roman Empire.[52]

Hellenism in Jewish Babylonia

In a very important discussion, Shaye Cohen has pointed to the Hellenism in Jewish Babylonia, noting that the very structuration of the rabbinic academies there, resembling the Hellenistic philosophical schools with their successions of "heads," is not to be found in rabbinic Palestine, and, therefore, "perhaps then the parallels between patriarchs and scholarchs tell us more about the Hellenization of Babylonian Jewry in the fourth and fifth centuries than about the Hellenization of Palestinian Jewry in the second."[53] This example supports the judgment of Cohen, albeit not in terms of Hellenistic influence, or even in terms of Hellenization; rather, I suggest that we consider Babylonian Jewish culture itself as a Hellenism, or more nuancedly, as a vibrant participant in Richard Kalmin's "rudiments of a partly shared elite culture [that] may have been emerging in Syria and Mesopotamia, perhaps a refinement of a rudimentary shared non-elite culture which had existed earlier."[54]

This emergence involves the development of a shared intellectual culture that flows through the Roman East and the Sasanian West.[55] In addition to the Sasanian one, we have to imagine multiple cultural contexts for the Talmud as a diasporic text.

Of Lemons and Languages

A story that has become a sort of locus classicus for the study of Iranian in Jewish Babylonia may help put flesh and bones on my proposed alternative mode of reading the Talmud as a diaspora.[56] The story is about as lively as it could get, but I'm going to treat in this context only a fragment from it. Rav Naḥman (as discussed above, the Babylonian Rabbi who asserts his discursive power even over Rabbi Yoḥanan, leader of the Palestinian community) has summoned Rav Yehuda, leader of another Babylonian Jewish community, to come see him over an alleged insult to one of his servants by the latter. Although from the rabbinic point of view, Rav Yehuda is of similar stature to Rav Naḥman, he has answered the subpoena owing to the special status of the latter as a member (by marriage) of the family of the exilarch, the temporal ruler of Jewish Babylonia. We enter the narrative upon Rav Yehuda's arrival:

> He found [Rav Naḥman] making a fence [*maʿaqe*]. He said, "Doesn't the master agree with what Rav Nahilai said in the name of Rav, that once one is appointed a leader of the people, it is forbidden [for him] to do manual labor in front of three others?"
>
> [Rav Naḥman] said: "I am just making a balustrade [*gundryza*]."
>
> He said to him: "Do you despise *maʿaqe*, which is written in the Torah, or *meḥiṣa*, as the Rabbis call it?!
>
> [Rav Naḥman] said to him: "Will the master sit down on a chaise [*qrpiṭa*]?"

> He said to him: "Is '*safsal*'—as the Rabbis say—hateful? Or ʾ*iṣṭeba*, as folk call it?"
> He said to him: "Would the master like to eat a citron [ʾ*itrunga*]?"
> He said to him: "Thus said Shmuel: One who says ʾ*itrunga* has one-third of arrogance in him. Either ʾ*etrog*, as the Rabbis call it, or ʾ*etroga*, as the people say!"
> He said to him: "Will the master drink some aperitif [ʾ*anbag*]?"
> He said: "Do you despise ʾ*ispargis*, as the Rabbis call it, or ʾ*anpaqa*, as the folk call it? (Kiddushin 70a)[57]

This story seemingly turns on a series of opaque linguistic differences. It begins with Rav Yehuda complaining that Rav Naḥman is doing manual labor in public, something that a rabbinic leader ought not to do, as it lowers the dignity of the office. This is some form of work, however, that the otherwise august and even arrogant Rav Naḥman feels is appropriate for him to do. I suggest very tentatively that the *maʿaqe* in question was the sort that one builds as a mitzvah, the performance of a commandment (one is enjoined to build a *maʿaqe* on a roof so that no one might fall off, as in Deut. 22:8). Rav Yehuda's initial question, therefore, is provocative; he knows exactly what Rav Naḥman is about. Had Rav Naḥman simply answered the question by saying, "I am building a *maʿaqe*," this conversation would have ended quickly (and happily), but Rav Naḥman chose to use some other—highfalutin and foreign—word rather than the ordinary biblical Hebrew one that names that commandment and its product. It is not surprising that Rav Yehuda found this off-putting. Elman has focused our attention on the fact that most of the terms used here by Rav Naḥman and objected to by Rav Yehuda are Iranian forms. He has interpreted the text, accordingly, as being the product of conflict between two cultural/political modes: one of accommodation to the dominating Persian culture (Rav Naḥman); and one of resistance (Rav Yehuda). Moreover, he locates these two modes respective to their places of residence: the former in the capital; the latter in the boondocks, where the language of the Sasanian overlords had not been introduced.[58] This interpretation is surely correct, but there is more to be said.

Militating against the monolithic interpretation of this story being about accommodation or resistance to Iranian culture remains the fact that some of Rav Naḥman's linguistic choices are not Iranian but Greek—for instance, the *qrpiṭa* κράβατος), his word for something to sit on. On the other hand, the word ascribed by the text to the people, *ʾiṣṭeba* (στιβας), is just as Greek as Rav Naḥman's word; it cannot be said that Greek is a class marker here, either. Another choice ascribed to the "Rabbis,"—that is, the Palestinians—the *ʾispargis*, is, once again, Greek, while both Rav Naḥman and "the people" use slightly different dialectal forms of the same Persian word. In the case of the citron, we have three different pronunciations of the same Persian word, the more Semitized Hebrew and Aramaic ones ascribed to the Rabbis and the people, respectively, while the more Persian-sounding one is condemned as arrogance or pretentiousness. This is clearly not just or even primarily a conflict over assimilation of Iranian lexical items in one's speech or even just of accommodation to Sasanian norms.

While Elman understands well that there is a class element here, noting that Rav Naḥman's speech is "upper-class Maḥozan," I think he doesn't sufficiently explicate that side of things or quite enough the alternatives that are offered by Rav Yehuda. It is not just a conflict between an urban and urbane elite versus a more parochial, rural one but also a deeply political conflict over the nature of Jewish culture, per se, that is limned here. This is encoded in the story in a bit that I did not cite here. Since he is of at least equal status to Rav Naḥman—say, the rough equivalent of a bishop of a different see—Rav Yehuda wonders whether he need respond to the latter's summons at all. A colleague whom he consults tells him that he needn't but should, nonetheless, in view of Rav Naḥman's close connections with the patriarchate, the exilarch of Babylonian Jews. Rav Naḥman, in summoning him this way, is employing his power (and prestige) in that extramural world to trump Rav Yehuda's in the world of Torah. This is thematized as well by Rav Naḥman's repeated use of these particular Persian and Greek words—specifically, ones that are not used by Jews—rather than the Persian, Greek, Hebrew, and Aramaic ones used in the Torah, by the Palestinian Sages, or by the Aramaic-speaking Jews of Babylonia and hence a sign of Rav Naḥman's arrogance (רמות רוחא). It is not so much Iranian culture that Rav Yehuda is resisting as much as Rav Naḥman and the multiply acculturated power structure to which he appeals and belongs. This interpretation is enhanced by the fact that in two of the instances, Rav Naḥman is not actually using different words but the same words pronounced with a Persian accent. Recall his arrogance toward Rabbi Yoḥanan in the previous section of this chapter, understood as issuing from his closeness to the exilarch (the Jewish overlord of the Jews of Babylonian appointed by the Sasanian rulers) and his family.[59]

I wish to underline, once more, the three linguistic contexts invoked by Rav Yehuda, as they together (with the addition of Rav Naḥman's "Persian") delineate the contours of the diasporic culture of the Talmud: biblical Hebrew, rabbinic Hebrew (as used in both Palestine and Babylonia), and Aramaic, the language of the folk.[60] Given that the Talmud marks, as we have seen in Chapter 2, that one of the explicit advantages of Babylonia for a Jewish "exile" was the fact that the language there is like the language of Torah, Rav Naḥman's abandoning of that language (he claims not to even understand Rav Yehuda's speech in the story) might well be taken as an abandonment of that diasporic ideal of shared Jewish language, a shared Jewish language marked as what the Bible, the Rabbis, or the people say. Note that the diasporic language is not uniform; it has elements of Greek (presumably, from its Palestinian "dialect") as well as elements of Persian; diaspora is signified by the absorption of local cultural goods and their circulation among Jews in other places. But Rav Naḥman here (not, I emphasize, the "historical" Rav Naḥman) insists on speaking a language that cuts him off from Jews in other times and climes.

Avant la lettre and not precisely, this conflict will help me distinguish between diaspora and cosmopolitanism (in its modern sense), observing Samir Dayal's stricture that there is "a particular danger . . . of facile and rootless cosmopolitanism masquerading as transvalued diaspora."[61] We can take Rav Naḥman as a figure for the cosmopolitan, remembering that the "citizen of the world" is always declaring him or herself a denizen of the world-dominant culture.[62] In this understanding, diaspora is directly opposed to cosmopolitanism, as diaspora retains and maintains the locale of the local as well as the trans-local, while cosmopolitanism dispenses entirely with the local: Rav Yehuda insists on the heteroglossia of biblical Hebrew (shared by all Jews), rabbinic Hebrew (shared by Rabbis in both places), and Aramaic (shared by Jews in Palestine and Babylonia, although with dialectal differences).

To be sure, the very terms "local" and "trans-local" are themselves oscillating, as vis-à-vis Babylonian Jewish culture, Iran is the local, Palestine the trans-local; while vis-à-vis the cosmopolitan culture, Iranian writ large is the trans-local and "Jewish" the local. Diaspora always produces a doubled consciousness that cosmopolitanism resists. Edward Said, I think, somewhat mislays this distinction when he writes: "Seeing 'the entire world as a foreign land' makes possible originality of vision. Most people are principally aware of one culture, one setting, one home; exiles are aware of at least two, and this plurality of vision gives rise to an awareness of simultaneous dimensions, an awareness that—to borrow a phrase from music—*is contrapuntal*."[63] Seeing the entire world as a foreign land is cosmopolitanism, but doubled cultural awareness is a different stance; it is being both located and not located within two places, two cultures at the same time. If doubled consciousness, what I call "diaspora"—not exile—is counterpoint, cosmopolitanism would be more analogous to the newest music that has no melody, no harmony, and no counterpoint at all (not meant as a condemnation, however; just playing out the analogy).

Once again, to come back to our talmudic narrative, some forms of "what the people say" are just as Iranian as what Rav Naḥman says—but

Semiticized. The "people" here are speakers of Aramaic, with its own stock of Iranian loanwords, more or less assimilated. More to the point, by suggesting—in a further unquoted incident in this story—that Rav Naḥman might be taken more than he ought to be with the upper-class, explicitly non-rabbinic, customs of the exilarch's house, a question is being raised as to his fitness to serve as a rabbinic leader and judge, as reflected in his wife's good advice to abandon the fray with Rav Yehuda before his reputation is entirely frayed.[64] It is not so much a question, therefore, of accommodation or resistance to a surrounding culture, as Elman would have it, but rather a question of to what surrounding culture we have reference: the Semitic/Aramaic one that binds Torah, Rabbis, and people and binds them to Palestine as well as to Babylonia (as the place where the language is like ours); or an exclusively upper-class Iranian one that divides between the Jews of Babylonia and the Jews of the Roman Empire. Rav Yehuda here is not so much the country bumpkin but the one who insists on the vitality of the linguistic/cultural ties with the Jews of Palestine, the Bible, the rabbinic, and the popular Aramaic, three of the key languages in the diasporic Jewish heteroglossia.

If we recall from the discussion above in this chapter that it was Rav Yehuda who insisted that it was forbidden to leave Babylonia to move to the Holy Land, this interpretation grows even stronger. By insisting, on the one hand, that Babylonian Jews must remain in Babylonia but, on the other hand, that they should speak languages that the Bible, the (Palestinian) Rabbis, and the Aramaic-speaking folk use, thus joining them linguistically/culturally to the Palestinian community, Rav Yehuda is the major site, if not the author, of a diasporist manifesto. In his extensive discussion of the final pages of tractate Ketubbot, Rubenstein shows that it is an extended Pumbeditan—the yeshiva founded by our Rav Yehuda—defense of Jewish life in Babylonia against the powerful traditional claims of the Holy Land.[65] We see, then, that in a deep sense, "diaspora" is exactly opposite to the usual terms of its description by historians and theologians. As diaspora is not—always—to be characterized as a deep and profound submission to the claims of a homeland, these diasporists insist on ties with the other Jews but resist the claim of anywhere but Babylonia to be a homeland.

It is in this sense that the Babylonian Talmud can be read as one of the literatures of the Roman Empire, despite the fact that it was produced on the eastern side of the limes. Secunda is cognizant of this point, although he theorizes it differently. Thus, in discussing the need (and the possibility) of contextualizing study of the Babylonian Talmud, he reminds us that "regarding textual remains, it should be recalled that talmudic commentators since medieval times have related the Bavli to Palestinian rabbinic literature. Parallels include Palestinian citations of Babylonian amoraim and stories set in Babylonia, both of which are either unattested in the Bavli, or appear in different versions."[66] He goes even further in this direction when he writes:

> More radically, growing sophistication regarding the way scholars understand how late antique texts were composed, redacted, and transmitted may allow for a more fluid approach to the geographic provenance of rabbinic texts. For example, it is possible that a particular passage in Ecclesiastes Rabbah is derived from earlier Babylonian material which traveled to Palestine, took on a new form, and was then further affected by the Bavli during later stages of its transmission. Related phenomena have been traced in the case of Avot de-Rabbi Nathan, and also apply to some of the biblical Targumim. It almost goes without saying that this approach is methodologically treacherous and should be employed with the utmost caution. Otherwise, we risk reversing the conclusions of textual taxonomies that have served the field well for many decades.[67]

If I have understood Secunda's final remark correctly, it seems that it is the taxonomy of Palestinian and Babylonian textual materials that we risk reversing. But it is the task of new research to question (not necessarily to reverse but certainly to interrogate) such taxonomies. There may be no doubt that the Iranian context for the Babylonian Talmud being uncovered lately is necessary for properly apprehending that unusual document. More than that, it is a necessary moment in the argument for the Talmud as a diasporic text, given my definition of diaspora as the cultural/social condition of a people oriented twice—to their locale and to another collective in another place. The Talmud is indeed a product of Sasanian Mesopotamia and, at the same time (not diachronically, but synchronically), a product of the trans-imperial rabbinic trans-culture.

Traveling Torah: The Locations of Talmud

In his recent book, *The Iranian Talmud*, Secunda develops a very sophisticated and convincing model for thinking about the kinds of textual relationships that he is documenting: "To conceive of these kinds of textual interactions, we might imagine a kind of late antique (and early medieval) 'text-scape' across Iranian lands that included, among other groups, Aramaic-speaking rabbis and Persian-speaking Zoroastrians. Using such a notion of a 'text-scape' may help account for related articulations appearing in different textual and cultural formations. It also implies that these phenomena might even represent a kind of textual interaction."[68] This is exceedingly elegantly formulated and useful, but why limit the application of this "text-scape" to Iranian lands when, for the Babylonian Rabbis, the text-scape surely includes the Greco-Aramaic-speaking East of the Roman Empire as well? It is not, of course, that Secunda denies the strong literary connections between the Bavli and Palestinian rabbinic literature, but he seems always to figure them as diachronic;[69] for him, the Bavli takes up Palestinian material and reuses it at a later time.[70] In my account, the relationships are synchronic with both Iranian and Palestinian languages (including Greek and

Syriac) as part of the text-scape, the intertextual world. In this example, we will see clearly that the relations of dependency don't go only one way; the Palestinian Talmud is as dependent on Babylonian materials as vice versa.

A Traveling Sugya; or, the Textual Making of a Diasporic Folk: Lighting the Lamp on Saturday Night

The first and foremost element of the "West" incorporated into their cultural, textual world was the ongoing traditions of learning in the part of the diaspora that they referred to as "the West": Palestine. The evidence for this assertion is, at first glance, so well known that it is hidden in plain sight. It can be found in the most everyday of talmudic genres, the halakhic sugya, to which I turn now. Our everyday sugya concerns the requirement to say a blessing on a lit flame on Saturday night at the end of the Sabbath as part of the ceremony of Havdalah, separating the sacred day and the profane days that follow. The Mishna says that one may not say this blessing over the light unless one has actually used the light: "A blessing is not said over the light until it has been used."

The talmudic discussion follows (Berakhot 53b): "Rav Yehuda said in the name of Rav: This does not mean literally until it has been used, but it means a light that could be usable were one standing near enough to it, and then even those at a distance [may say the blessing]. So, too, said Rav Asi:[71] We have learned that even those at a distance may make the blessing."

A tradition is cited in the name of the Babylonian amora Rav Yehuda in the name of his teacher Rav that this should not be taken too literally but rather is descriptive of the type of light that is required: a light that would be serviceable were one near it, but one does not have to be actually near it in order to bless. This statement is then contested in classical talmudic form by citing a tannaitic [pre-rabbinic] tradition:

"They object: 'If he had a candle hidden in his cloak or in a lamp or if he saw the flame but did not use its light or used its light but did not see the flame, he may not bless until he sees the flame and uses the light.'"

The Talmud goes on to explicate the objection: "It makes sense that one can use the light without seeing the flame—for instance, if it is around the corner; but how can you see the flame and not use the light? Isn't it only if you are distant from it?" Therefore, since this authoritative early source says that one may not bless under such circumstances, it would seem that Rav Yehuda and Rav Asi are refuted in their claim that one may bless even on seeing the flame at a distance. The refutation is, however, refuted: "No, it is a case in which it is the flame that becomes dim."

The objection to Rav Yehuda is thus displaced. The tannaitic statement that says that one may not bless on a light where one sees the flame but cannot use it is not about distance from the flame but a case where one is near, but the flame is flickering and going out, thus restoring Rav Yehuda's claim about distance by refuting the refutation. This refutation of the refutation is then supported by the following: "Our Rabbis teach: one may make a blessing on coals that are glowing but not on coals that are dim [*ʿomemot*]. What is the definition of 'glowing'? Rav Ḥisda said any that, if you place a stick of kindling among them, would light itself."

This tradition supports the idea that it is in the case where the flames are going out and merely flickering, not glowing, that one may not make the blessing; but if the flames are big, even from a distance and not really using the flame, one may make the blessing in accordance with the view of Rav Yehuda in the name of Rav.

After a bit of some further philological byplay, the text goes on with the citation of an entirely different opinion as to the meaning of the Mishna. The amora Rava insists that it is to be taken literally: "But Rava said: It means literally that the light has been used." The passage goes on to ask a question seemingly governed by Rava's statement: "How much?" As Rashi reads it, the question is: "How near must he be [to the light in order to bless on it]?" In other words, according to Rashi's interpretation, even Rava doesn't talk about actual use but about the necessity to be near the light; even for him, it is the potential for use and not actual use that is at issue.

In answer to the question "How much / How near," we find two answers: "'Ulla said: Enough to distinguish between an *issar* and a *pundion* [two Greek, that is, Palestinian, coins, the *pundion* (*dupundion*) double in value and size to the *issar* (*as*)]." Two small coins, one of which is double the other in size, and thus apparently relatively easier to tell apart than the next opinion. "Ḥizkia said: Enough to distinguish between a *meluzma* [*numisma*] of Tiberias and one of Sepphoris." This is a stricter rule than the previous one, for now we are talking about the same coin, or weight, only with the slight differences that obtain when it is minted in one city or another, so it would seem that more light is involved than 'Ulla's opinion would imply, as presumably, we have to read the legend or decipher the iconography of the coins to tell one from the other. Both these Rabbis, following Rava's statement, indicate, as Rashi reads the text, that one must be very near—without necessarily using the light—near enough that one *could* use it for this or for that purpose of distinguishing coins.

The Talmud goes on to tell us the practices of various Rabbis who apparently followed the rule of Rav Yehuda and Rav Asi that one could bless on the light from a distance, that it has to be enough light to use were one near but that one does not actually have to use it: "Rav Yehuda would bless on the [light from] the house of Rav Adda the steward; Rava would bless on the [light from] the house of Gurya the son of Ḥama; Abbaye would bless on the [light from] the house of Bar Avuha."

These three amoraim are reported to have said the blessing on passing the lit-up houses of various important(?) folk in their neighborhoods on Saturday night, and thus, at any rate seemingly not to have looked too hard for a candle or lamp that they could get near, still less make actual use thereof. This impression is then ratified by the final statement of our little sugya: "Rav Yehuda said in the name of Rav: One does not have to search diligently for a light [to bless upon] as one searches diligently to fulfill commandments. Rabbi Zeʿira said: I used to search diligently, but once I heard this saying of Rav Yehuda in the name of Rav, I, too, don't search diligently. Rather, if I happen by chance on a light, I bless." Although this sugya seems quite simple, we will discover that it is actually an intricately composed and structured little document and that its complications are highly revealing of the Talmud's cultural entailments. It is the question of the Babylonian-ness or Palestinianhood of the speakers and their views that will enable us to see the complexities.

Let me recapitulate the flow of the sugya, paying attention this time to the location of the various speakers. The first amoraic speaker is a Babylonian whom we have met earlier as the antagonist of Rav Naḥman: Rav Yehuda, the leading disciple of the great Rav, who brought the Mishna to Babylonia and in his name. Rav Yehuda declares that when the Mishna says (as it clearly does) that one may only say this blessing after having made use of the light, that's not what it really means; it means that it has to be a light that would be usable were one near enough to it. A later Babylonian authority, Rava, then declares that Rav Yehuda is wrong; the Mishna must be taken literally, and it must be a light that has been actually used for something (the point being, presumably, that by using the light, one signifies the new freedom to use fire after the prohibition on that usage for the Sabbath).

We then ask a puzzling question: "How much?"—How much what, precisely? It would seem from the context following Rava's statement that the question is "How much use constitutes use?" But the way the textus receptus has placed these statements before the practices of the three Rabbis who seemingly would bless at a distance, the question, as Rashi reads it, seems to be how near must he be even if he is not himself using it. By ordering the statements in this way, the author of the sugya (the *stam*) has produced an ambiguity in their view: Do they or do they not require actual usage of the light? These two Palestinian amoraim, one of whom, ʿUlla, we have met above in his guise of traveler, and another named Ḥizkia, declare, respectively, that he needs to be near enough to distinguish either a somewhat large difference—say, as between a nickel and a dime; or enough to make successfully a tiny distinction—say, between a French euro coin and a German one. The sugya goes on to give us reports of a series of Babylonian amoraim who used to bless as they passed various houses, or as they looked out the window at such houses from their own, and concludes by coming back to a statement of Rav Yehuda in the name of Rav, again to the effect that the whole business of this blessing is fairly optional and aleatory. If you happen to see such a light, you bless; if not, not, as opposed to other commandments that you are expected to go out of your way to fulfill. We conclude with a report about a disciple of Rav Yehuda who, upon hearing this report from his teacher, puts it into practice and becomes much less ardent about fulfilling this commandment.

As I have laid it out, the sugya provides fairly elaborate support primarily for the view of Rav Yehuda in the name of Rav that one does not have to actually use the candle in order to make this blessing. Even the statements of the two Palestinians, ʿUlla and Ḥizkia, are made also to be about how near one needs to be, not about actual usage of the candle for some purpose. Rava's view seems a bit confused, however. On the one hand, he is represented as demanding literal usage of the light; on the other, as making the blessing even on passing a certain house and seeing the light within. This is resolved in various ways by commentators: Rashi remarks that the house of this Gurya was very near Rava's house, thus supporting his view; others say that the one who blessed on passing the house of Gurya was another authority entirely, the amora with the similar name, Rabbah.

Note, especially, how local are the knowledges referred to in all instances. To make sense of this sugya, we need, on the one hand, to know the sizes of Roman coins and even of the differences between various localized Palestinian weights and measures; on the other hand, we need to know the precise location of these particular houses in Babylonia. As we've just seen, interpreters are more or less left to guess (as Rashi did and as I have) as to these relationships from the text and on the basis of our attempts to make sense of it. The fact remains that the text is embedded in two different historical realities and sets of realia, thus dramatizing, on my definition, its diasporic nature. One could even imagine that it is this dual location that is almost the main point of these bi-local points of reference to the "real world." The world of Tiberias and Caesarea Maritima and the world of Sura, Maḥoza, Nehardea, and Pumbedita are rendered one world via this text, paralleling the phenomenon of men in the Talmud carrying on conversations across hundreds of miles and distinct generations.

The story of this sugya is not yet all told. As I have read it till now, the two Palestinian Rabbis are engaged in the same discourse ("How far"?) as the Babylonian Rabbis for whom the question of distance has been raised by Rav Yehuda in the name of Rav and by Rav Asi, his Babylonian contemporary. This comes out from the placement of their two statements just before those of the Babylonians, who are said to have blessed on light seen from other houses. If we take them out of that context, it is possible to read the two Palestinians as having a different agenda entirely: not how near or how far, but how much actual use constitutes use. On that reading, which I will support presently, they didn't even know anything about Rav Yehuda's (Babylonian) agenda of reducing the importance of this ceremony by allowing blessing at a distance from the source of light and also the same Rabbi's saying that one does not have to put much effort into fulfilling it. They would simply be commenting on the Mishna according to its simple meaning, never even put into question by them or for them. You have to make actual use of the light before you can make a blessing about it, and they ask: What constitutes using?

There is at least one manuscript of the Babylonian Talmud in which this is explicit. The text there reads:[72] "One does not bless on the candle until one has used its light. [Not have used] literally, but rather as much so that if one were standing near, one could use its light; but even if one is standing at a distance, since the light reaches him, he may bless. Rav

Asi also said, we have taught [this Mishna] as referring to a distant place." At this point, there comes the objection and resolution as we have seen above, and then, immediately: "*How much need they make use of the light?* ʿUlla said, until he can distinguish between pale blue and white, between an *issar* and a *pundion*. Ḥizkia said, until he can distinguish between a *meluzma* of Tiberias and a *meluzma* of Sepphoris. Rava said, makes use, literally."

According to this textual witness, the question "How much" is not about how near or how far, as it is in the textus receptus and according to Rashi's commentary, but clearly about actual employment of the light. In other words, in this version of the text, it is explicit that the two Palestinian Rabbis are not aware of the idea that one might not actually have to use the light to make this blessing. They assume that one has to make actual use of it (which is, after all, the straightforward sense of the Mishna); they are concerned only with how much use constitutes use. The Babylonian Rava is cited following them as explicitly demanding literal use, since his Babylonian predecessor had denied this, but the Palestinians are not aware of such a possibility. This is followed by the statement of not being required to seek after a light to bless: "Rav Yehuda said in the name of Rav: One does not have to search diligently for a light [to bless upon] as one searches diligently to fulfill commandments. Rabbi Zeʿira said: I used to search diligently, but once I heard this saying of Rav Yehuda in the name of Rav, I, too, don't search diligently. Rather, if I happen by chance on a light, I bless, but I don't look for one."[73]

Only now comes the report about the practices of the various Babylonian amoraim: "Rav Yehuda blessed on the [light from the] house of Ada the steward; Abbaye blessed on the [light from the] house of Gurya the son of Ḥama; Rava blessed on the [light from] the house of Bar Ḥabu."

The point of this report according to this setup of the sugya is to indicate support for Rav Yehuda's view that one need not seek a light to make this blessing but that on happening to pass a light during one's usual activity, one makes the blessing. There is no indication of how near or far one needs to be or of whether actual use has been made of this light.

So what do I make of all this? First, we see the sugya as a work in progress during its manuscript journeys; bits and pieces of the text have migrated to different locations within it. Second, we see that the textus receptus, found not only in the first print but also in a couple of other manuscripts, represents a tendentious rearranging of materials to assimilate the views of the two Palestinian authorities, ʿUlla and Ḥizkia, to the question of how near or far he must be from the light to bless. We see that their question was originally: How much use must one make? But it has been transformed in the later talmudic versions into how near one must be to the light, regardless of whether he makes use of it. Furthermore, by placing the report on the practices of the three Babylonian Rabbis where it has been placed in the textus receptus, it is made to support the view that one may bless on a light seen from a distance and need not use it.

Support for the suggestion that in Palestine, they knew nothing of attempts to downgrade this observance by saying that it could be done at a long distance from the light comes from the parallel Talmud, the Palestinian Talmud (and we're in for a bit of a surprise):

> One does not bless on the candle until one uses its light.
>
> Rav Yehuda in the name of Shmuel: Sufficient for women to spin in its light. Rabbi Yoḥanan said: Sufficient such that his eye could see what is in a cup or a bowl. Rav Ḥinena said: Sufficient for him to distinguish between one coin and another.
>
> Rabbi ʿOshaya taught: One may bless even in a hall that is ten by ten.
>
> Rabbi Zeʿira would bring the candle near himself. His pupils said to him: Rabbi, why are you being so strict for us [that is, setting such a strict example for us to follow]? Didn't Rabbi ʿOshaya teach that one may bless even in a hall that is ten by ten?[74]

One might have been tempted to imagine that the Babylonian version of the sugya is a (tendentious or non-tendentious) rewriting of the Palestinian material, except for the surprise. The first voice cited in the Palestinian text is the Babylonian Rav Yehuda, who is taking, it would seem, the opposite view from the one he expresses in the Babylonian Talmud. Here he seems to know nothing of a nonliteral reading of the Mishna and simply participates in the discussion of how much constitutes usage of the light. Rabbi Yoḥanan, his—of course—Palestinian coeval, is made to participate in this conversation with him, although, of course, this could not have been face-to-face.[75] The view that one needs to be able to distinguish one coin from another is cited neither in the name of ʿUlla nor in the name of Ḥizkia but in the name of Ḥinena. This Rav Ḥinena—as his title Rav, not Rabbi—would suggest, was a Babylonian as well and a close disciple of Rav. He, too, seems to know nothing of a tradition in the name of his teacher and Rav Yehuda's that one need not make use of the light at all. In other words, Rav Yehuda's (and maybe Rav's own) views as cited in the Palestinian Talmud are the opposite of those in the Babylonian. Fascinatingly, when the opinion is given in the Bavli, in the name of the Palestinian, specific Palestinian realia are referenced, while in the Palestinian Talmud, we are given the neutral "between one coin and another." Rabbi Zeira (aka Zeʿira) comes in here as well but in a different guise. He did, as in the Bavli, have a strict practice with respect to this blessing that he apparently lightened up afterward. It is the Palestinian tanna Rabbi ʿOshaya who is the support for this more lenient view but not anything as lenient as the Babylonian Talmud would have it. Neither at a distance nor by chance; all that Rabbi ʿOshaya permits is blessing on a light when one is in the same room as that light and not right on top of it. Where did this conversation between Rabbi Zeira and his students take place? We don't know, since he was a Babylonian who migrated to Palestine.

This is, indeed, a traveling sugya. At both ends of its journey, it constructs a world in which Babylonian and Palestinian Rabbis are in the same virtual room—but with a difference. The Palestinian room with its Babylonian visitors does not know of a nonliteral reading of the

Mishna, or of a casual attitude toward fulfilling the commandment of making this blessing at the conclusion of the Sabbath. My intuition—and it's not much more than that—is that the Palestinian Talmud has the more original form of the traditions in the name of Rav and his disciples, and the Babylonian has redacted not only the Palestinian but also the Babylonian views for its own purposes. The most lenient the Palestinian Talmud gets on this issue is allowing one to bless on a light that one sees in the same room. The Babylonian Talmud quite tendentiously pushes the commandment away; one does not need literally to use or come near the light, and one does not need to seek a light out (with the exception of the voice of Rava, an ambiguously lone voice in the standard texts, supported by the Palestinians in the earlier manuscripts of the Bavli and by the Palestinian Talmud). This Rava is consistent with himself, as he is reported in Pesaḥim 8a as saying that a "torch for Havdalah is of the choicest of mitzvot." I suspect, although I would not want to insist too strenuously, that it is that Iranian text-scape that Elman and his students have revealed to us that explains this difference—it has something to do with the sacrality of fire among the Zoroastrian overlords of Babylonia that is at work here, but I would not want to speculate as to what the factor is.[76] I hope that this case study of a sugya—chosen at random and not atypical—has helped to nail down the case that I do want to make here strenuously of the talmudic culture being a diaspora and the Talmuds themselves diasporic in their dual simultaneous locations of local Babylonia/Palestine, respectively, and the other place where Rabbis study Torah.

At the end of his book, Gafni comes almost all the way to rethinking diaspora completely. Comparing the two stories of the intercalation of the calendar by Rabbi Ḥananiah that I have presented above, as told in the Palestinian and in the Babylonian Talmud, he demonstrates that for the former, Palestine is always and immutably the site of calendrical intercalations and thus always and immutably the site of rabbinic power, while in the Babylonian story, whichever of the two communities has more recognition as the most learned in talmudic studies is the center (and even the virtual Holy Land). For the Babylonians, then, diaspora is constituted via a cultural connection and cultural authority and not on the basis of an originary Homeland. It may be the case that, as Gafni claims, most of the stories about the transfer of Torah traditions represent the learning as coming from Palestine to Babylonia but the facts on the ground of the text suggest otherwise; all those citations of Babylonian Rabbis (to be sure, fairly early ones) have to have come from somewhere. Gafni clearly understands, as well, that the processes of diasporization are not once and for all. First, the Babylonians imagine, construct Babylonia as Zion, as we have seen earlier; but later, others take the Babylonian Talmud and with it construct other later diasporas: "The process we have encountered here would repeat itself throughout Jewish history: new communities would rise up and assert themselves vis-à-vis their mother communities, and this 'breaking away' would be painful for both centers."[77]

Or not, as it happens. Nothing in the narrative of the four captives seems to indicate pain for the breakaways. This seems a bit of projection; neither do the Rabbis of the Babylonian Talmud—with a few exceptions—manifest pain at the breaking away from the Palestinian authority. It is not breaking away so much that is at stake (although it can be—explicitly so, in the narrative of the four captives) as the constitution of culturally equal partnerships that necessitates shared culture. I suggest that this is precisely a point of the Babylonian sugya as a form. It constructs a readership that is not quite *in* either place but in both simultaneously, a diasporic subject, subject of the Land of Talmud, in which Tiberias and Pumbedita are integral parts of the same locale. The Talmud, as Christina von Braun has written, rendered the Jewish people *diasporafähig*,[78] capable and worthy of diaspora. In the next and final chapter, I explore the routes of Talmud study in the Middle Ages and early modern periods (did Jews have a Middle Ages or a Renaissance?), showing how the Talmud as diaspora produces a bifocal Jewish culture shared ultimately by the Jews of Eastern Europe, Western Europe, and the Balkan lands, as well as North Africa, Mesopotamia, and Syria.

Chapter 4

Looking for Our Routes; or, the Talmud and the Making of Diasporas: Sefarad and Ashkenaz

> All the subdivisions of the people, the literary Sefardi, the philosophical Provençal, the mystical Ashkenazi, and the ingenuous Eastern—all of them had a common denominator: investigating and interpreting the Talmud, in addition to their own individual intellectual world.
>
> —Hayyim Zalman Dimitrovsky[1]

This little book began with a story of a ship that was sailing from Bari,[2] carrying, at least metaphorically, the Talmud in the form of four scholars who would found four new—three of them real and one of them "unknown" and thus totally imaginary—and ultimately great centers of talmudic learning at the four corners of the known Mediterranean, producing a new diaspora: "From Bari the Torah will go out, and the word of the Lord from Otranto." As I noted in Chapter 1, the author of this account, Rabbi Avraham Ibn Daud, the great defender of the talmudic tradition and rhetorical founder of its new diaspora in the Arabic world, was also known as "Avendauth who cooperated with Dominicus Gundissalinus in translating philosophical texts from Arabic into

Latin,"[3] as well as being the founder of Jewish[4] Aristotelian philosophy, the dominant current of which culminated in such figures as Maimonides, who also combined great talmudic learning with world-class achievement in philosophy: true diasporic men. It is hardly my brief here to account for Ibn Daud—still less, for Maimonides—as a figure in intellectual history. I will use Ibn Daud rather as an emblem of the cultural productivity of my model and definition of "diaspora," moving forward to another spectacular instance of a Jewish diaspora that is characterized by its cultural openness and fecundity in spreading a new culture to other Jewish collectives, thus reproducing once more the cultural creativity that is diaspora.[5]

The Ways of Talmud

Talmudic study is proverbial for a logic-chopping intensely dialectical practice, but these intensely dialectical methods in which the interpretation of Talmud matched the Talmud in its style were invented as an integral part of medieval intellectual developments in the Rhineland involving an intense textualization of Christian and Jewish societies. These scholastic practices then came from Ashkenaz to Sefarad, where previously, the Talmud had been studied primarily to extract normative halakha and, as such, only by specialists in that field. As Talya Fishman has well noted: "[U]p until the thirteenth century (when Naḥmanides and his students imported the tosafist [dialectical] method of Talmud study, thereby 'homogenizing' the rabbinic world), Talmud played different roles in the lives of Sefardi and Ashkenazi Jews."[6] Thus major components of talmudic culture were developed in the Rhineland as part of textualizing developments within general culture there.[7] These developments within Ashkenaz and their arrival with Naḥmanides in Sefarad provided one of the necessary, but not sufficient, conditions for the development of the special early modern modes of talmudic study that came into being in the fifteenth century, the other being the Aristotelian epistemology of the Muslim world, within which the Sefardim flourished.[8]

Rabbi Yitzḥak Kanpanton, the last rabbi of Iberian Jewry before the Expulsion of 1492 and founder of the new method, devoted much of his effort as a logical interpreter to the northern French Rashi, on the one hand, and to the texts of Naḥmanides, on the other. In other words, Greco-Arabic logical analysis was now joined to the interpretation of northern European, scholastic dialectic, as the regnant method of talmudic study. It is compelling to me that the later flowering of talmudic study in the Ashkenazi world, the methods of study that became famous (and infamous) under the name of *pilpul*, were the product of the recirculation into northern Europe of the Aristotelian culture of talmudic study that had developed in Sefarad. Otherwise, it is extraordinarily difficult to explain how terms that are only explicable as Hebrew calques of Arabic calques of Greek would have reached them at all, in Mainz, Regensburg, Nürnberg, Kraków, and Lublin.

As we have seen, Abraham Ibn Daud, near the beginning of the Golden Age for Spanish Jewry, combines easily in himself an intellectual life that is dedicated to the promulgation of the Babylonian Talmud and also is a major voice in Jewish philosophy, as well as a translator of Arabic philosophy into Latin. Shmuel Hannagid continues such a way of life, contributing to the political life of Granada as well as being central for Hebrew poetry and even more for talmudic interpretation and halakha. Maimonides, in this tradition as well, is certainly the capital articulation of Jewish Aristotelianism but also arguably the most important interpreter of Talmud of his day (both sides of his work are studied avidly and widely until today). Less well known is the continuing influence that the Aristotelian tradition had on Spanish and Sefardic Jewish intellectual life in the fifteenth and sixteenth centuries, including its most particularly Jewish of activities, the interpretation of the Talmud. In this period, there appears Kanpanton's new theory and practice of talmudic hermeneutic, which is called *ʿiyyun*, "speculation"—talmudic interpretation as an application of the Aristotelian theory of language.[9]

In the earlier stages of Sefardic culture, the so-called Golden Age, we observe, as in Maimonides, two parallel tracks of cultural activity; in this "Silver Age," the two tracks have been brought together: Talmud study has been made a branch of philosophical investigation. After seeing how this mode of interpretation, invented on Spanish soil in the fifteenth century, integrates the two sides of this great Sefardic culture, we will follow its routes in the Sefardic communities after the Expulsion and even before that in Central and Eastern Europe, as it produces yet again a new diaspora, one that we might call the diaspora of *pilpul* (lit., peppering), the name for the particular hermeneutic practices thus promulgated. *Pilpul* is definable best as extremely close (sometimes excessively close) attention to the logic and necessity of every word and every move in the talmudic argument. This new diaspora, as the previous ones, has a doubled cultural location. In Arabic and some Christian lands (Provence, Italy), it is thoroughly embedded in the local intellectual life of Aristotelian (and other) philosophy and also thoroughly imbued with the transcultural and trans-local practice of the study of Talmud. In its transfer into the Christian cultural world of northern and then northeastern Europe, it is the means by which Aristotle's ideas about language, as mediated through Arabic translations and philosophical writings, are brought into that Jewish cultural world, thus revitalizing the study of Talmud wherever it traveled.

The most important methodological work of the school of *ʿiyyun* is *Darkhe hatalmud* (The Ways of Talmud), by the father of the method, R. Yitzḥak Kanpanton (d. 1463, Castille),[10] together with his chief disciple, Rabbi Yitzḥak Aboab (the second; d. 1493, Portugal),[11] the last great intellectual leaders of Spanish Jewry before the Expulsion. Studying this text enables us to discern different scholastic modes of thinking and expression at work in it.

Kanpanton's greatest achievement was the revival of talmudic learning as an important intellectual pursuit of the Iberian Jewish intelligentsia, after nearly a century during which this pursuit was not highly regarded. It can reasonably be hypothesized that one reason he was so successful in this endeavor was his ability to express talmudic learning in the language of the scholastic philosophical discourse so highly regarded by that very intelligentsia and to show that talmudic logic was, in many respects, comparable with Aristotelian logic or, more specifically, Aristotelian linguistic doctrine. His method of interpreting the Talmud became, through his disciples who founded yeshivot throughout the Ottoman Empire, the dominant method of study and interpretation in the Sefardic diaspora for the two centuries following the Expulsion.

Sophistical Refutations: From Aristotle to Rashi

One of the most misunderstood elements of Kanpanton's method already in its own time was the insistence on producing false interpretations of the talmudic text, only to disprove them in the end. This was misconstrued by contemporaries and near-contemporaries as a merely academic show of prowess and roundly attacked by various rabbinic figures as mere sophistry. This method had, however, several sound bases in the logical thought of the later Middle Ages. The first has to do with the reason that interpretation is necessary, in Kanpanton's view. In a key passage, he states: "Alternatively, the commentator will interpret the matter, in order to exclude another opinion or another interpretation, which would be possible in the potentiality of the language, for, according to the simple meanings of the words and the syntax, it would be possible to err and entertain another view. In order to guard against that and drive it out from the minds of the *me'ayyenim* (since in truth, it is a falsehood): that is the reason he interprets."[12]

The key phrases in Kanpanton's explication are all couched in the language of Hebrew Aristotelianism. The most important phrase is "possible in the potentiality of the language [*beko'aḥ hallašon*]," that is, what is possible to understand as a potential—but erroneous—interpretation of the language of the text. The phrase "potentiality of the language" is accordingly similar in force to *sebara mibbaḥuẓ.*[13] To put it differently, the single verbal proposition is equivocal; its language has the potential to be understood in more than one way.

Equivocation in the Middle Ages is defined as a single verbal proposition being subordinated to more than one mental proposition. This generally results from the polysemous nature of terms within the proposition. For most medieval semanticists—Roger Bacon is perhaps an exception—the meanings of polysemous or homonymous terms are fixed: they have been fixed by an "imposition," or a series of impositions, on the part of the ancient peoples. Thus we find in Maimonides' logical writings the following definition of the Hebrew word for "speech": "The word 'dibbur' is a homonymous term by imposition of the ancient peoples, which signifies three intentions. The first is that faculty, by which man is distinguished, with which he conceives concepts (intelligibles) and learns sciences and distinguishes between the contemptible and the appropriate. This intention is also called 'the faculty of speech' or 'the speaking soul.' The second intention is the concept, already conceived by the man. This intention is called 'the inner speech.' The third intention is the utterance in speech of the intention (concept) impressed upon the soul. This intention is also called 'the outer speech.'"[14]

Therefore, a given proposition in a text has a limited number of possible interpretations, of which the parameters are the various possibilities that are potential in each of its terms. One function of determining possible false readings of the text, then, is to show the necessity for the comment of the interpreter as excluding those false readings that exist in the potential of the language.

Kanpanton's doctrine is explicitly connected (by his terminology) to the scholastic analysis of sophisms or fallacies. His use of the terms "err" and "to guard against" in the above citation point in this direction, for both are terms of art of the Hebrew literature on sophisms. Most revealing is Kanpanton's use of the term "sophisms" or "fallacies" (*haṭaʿot* = modern Hebrew *haṭayot*) to mean the false interpretations of a passage rejected by the canonical commentators. Sophisms were analyzed by

Aristotle into two types: "sophisms in speech"; and those "out of speech"—or, in the terminology of Hebrew scholasticism, *haṭaʿot ašer bammillot* and *haṭaʿot ašer baʿinyanim*. Clearly, Kanpanton is referring to sophisms of speech, defined as the fallacious acceptance of one of the possible significations of an equivocal expression, when, in fact, another is correct. By referring to the incorrect, rejected interpretations as *haṭaʿot*, he is drawing an analogy between the commentator and logician, whose common job is to teach people to "guard themselves" from the snares of seductive fallacy.

The great logician Abū Naṣr Muḥammad ibn Muḥammad Al-Farabi (tenth century) defined the purpose of logic as giving "rules common to all languages, by which outer speech is guided toward what is correct, and guarded against error," which, in Hebrew, yields *yišmerehu min haṭṭaʿut*. It is hardly surprising, therefore, that what a commentator does is referred to in all branches of *pilpul* by the root *šmr*—for example, Rashi *nišmar mizze* (guarded against this), and the *pilpul* method of analyzing commentaries is called universally, in Sefarad and Ashkenaz alike, *derek hašemirot* (the method of guarding).

We can see that the setting up of false interpretations is an integral part of the system of thought and interpretation of R. Yitzḥak and his followers. These false interpretations are required to show why it was necessary for a commentator to comment at all, by showing the sophisms possible in the text and to serve as proof for the ineluctability of his interpretation. The lengths gone to show the plausibility of the false interpretations served the first purpose, for if there be no true *causa apparentia*, there is no true fallacy—hence no need to interpret. Moreover, it is necessary to eliminate all possible sophisms to prove that only one interpretation is possible and therefore correct. Dialectical sophistry is thus conceived of as the only way to achieve truth and certainty in exegesis. As Kanpanton remarks: "The truth cannot be known, except through its opposite."

This view was not merely an eccentricity of talmudists but was deeply embedded in the epistemology of its time and place, and this is precisely my point here. The fifteenth-century Spanish Jewish philosopher and logician Abraham Shalom articulates it when he says: "A man is not called a hero of wisdom, until he can demonstrate a proposition two ways, once positively and once negatively, for a matter is only known through its opposite."[15] It is surely no coincidence that Shalom uses the term "ways," *derakim*, a technical term of *ʿiyyun* as well, meaning the alternative interpretations possible in the text.[16] The ultimate seriousness of this philosophy can be shown by citing two contemporaneous texts.

The first, by R. Yitzḥak Aboab, claims that God uses the method of sophisms to teach humans the truth; he explains by this principle the age-old question of why the Mishna enunciates wrong opinions together with correct ones: "All of them were given by the same shepherd (Ecclesiastes 12). He wants to say that most often we understand a matter well only via its opposite, and we understand it from its opposite; and, therefore, the Holy One, blessed be He, wished to give us the differing opinions, so that when we arrived at the truth, we would understand it clearly."[17] The necessity of dealing in falsehood, of setting up and knocking down fallacies, is a feature of the human condition. Only one to whom truth is vouchsafed by revelation can escape it.

The second text is expressed beautifully by another of Kanpanton's disciples, R. Joseph Taitazak: "The influence of blessed God was so great upon Adam that he knew the truth without struggle or effort, and everything was before him like a set table. As for primordial Adam, since the truth grew by itself, there was not need to weed out and cut down the false divisions [*ḥaluqot*], for they were cut down of themselves."[18]

But for all of us post-Adamic creatures, the only way to arrive at truth is by systematically eliminating falsehood. This was the practice of talmudic interpreters—Sefardic and, later, Ashkenazic—who developed elaborate methods for setting up every imaginable way of interpreting the talmudic passage and knocking down all but one. It is, once again, important to put all these techniques in their original context in a particular epistemology, lest they remain open to the misunderstandings (willy-nilly) of those who do not see the serious intellectual import of such practices as building elaborate edifices and then knocking them down. In a very colorful manner, one contemporary opponent of this method wrote: "And in the *derakim* that you will argue about until the end of your days, raising interpretative possibilities and knocking them down, you call this craft *pilpul* but I call it *bilbul* [confusion]."[19] I am reminded of an incident early in my teaching career when I spent half the lecture explaining the view of another scholar on some matter, and then said, but in my opinion, this is an unsatisfactory explanation—only to be asked by an undergraduate whether he could erase it from his notebook.[20]

Clearly, a major principle of talmudic interpretation of Yitzḥak Kanpanton is simply a fundamental epistemological principle of his time and place, brilliantly applied to the discipline of talmudic hermeneutics. One way of thinking of this is to use a biological metaphor. Organisms evolve in response to their environment, making themselves more adapted to a given environment; fascinatingly, this is called "ecotypification," a term adapted by ethnographers and folklorists to refer to the local adaptations of shared cultural materials.[21] What we've observed is talmudic study adapting itself, learning from its environment (not being influenced passively but actively learning and developing). It is the diasporic condition of being in two cultures at once that is so productive. Cultural actors who were, in this case, intimately involved with Arabic (and Latin) scholasticism were able to refine and develop new ways of studying the Talmud, which had a revitalizing effect on that study not only in their place but, owing to the cultural connection with other Jewish collectives of talmudic study, throughout the Mediterranean, the Ottoman Empire, and also into the Ashkenazi talmudic cultures of Germany and Eastern Europe.[22]

Polysystems and the Jewish Question

Most "science of Judaism" research is carried out under a paradigm of the Jews as a separate cultural entity whose presence in other cultures is abnormal (from the point of view of Jewish existence). Such interaction between Jewish and circumambient culture as I have documented can only be accounted for as influence from the surroundings. This paradigm is generated by a particular cultural ideology and is less than perspicacious for describing facts on the ground and self-understanding of those cultural actors. An example: Shall that same Shmuel Hannagid, vizier of Granada, be described as acting under Arabic influence when he writes his poetry, or shall he be better described as a doubled cultural actor, local and trans-local at once? Should Rabbi Yitzḥak Kanpanton be described as under Greek or Arabic influence in developing his method of studying the Talmud and interpreting it, or should he be described as mobilizing his doubled cultural location and thus producing something new? A more appropriate model is that of the polysystem, studying the ways in which specifically Jewish cultural practices, such as Talmud study, interact with other signifying practices in which Jews and others are involved together. When the polysystem includes—as we have seen that talmudic culture does—local and trans-local systems at once, we have a diaspora.

The concept of the polysystem, a product of the "Tel Aviv" school of poetics, sees culture (and the products of culture) not as a closed signifying system but as the interaction at the same time of different signifying practices and systems that are all current within the culture.[23] This dynamic is what allows for cultural change and renewal, for the different systems within the culture interpenetrate and modify one another. An excellent example of this process from an area entirely different from what we are studying would be the way that jazz developed in American culture out of the interaction between American and African musical traditions and ultimately fructified even the practice of "classical" music-making in America, such as in the work of George Gershwin—that diasporic Jew. This dynamic is not understood on polysystem theory as a special case but as the typical and ever-present process of cultural creation and development. Go one step further with this analogy, and the forging of ties between different communities around the

"Black Atlantic" on the basis of sharing these musical practices becomes the perfect model of diaspora as I conceive it. It is the interplay of doubled cultural location within culture actors and collectives that is the mark of diaspora—not influence on putatively enclosed systems.

It would be extremely misleading were we to speak of Islamic or Spanish influences on the work or persons of such figures as the Nagid or Maimonides. They are Spaniards contributing to and participating in Ibero-Arabian culture as fully and as importantly as any other figures in medieval Spanish history. At the same time, much of their cultural practice is specifically Jewish in content, whether halakhic, hermeneutic, theological, or poetic. In order for us to see the one part of their work as authentic and Spanish and the other part as Jewish work influenced by Spanish culture, we have to schizophrenize them, split them into two distinct personalities. There is not a shred of evidence for such split personalities in the Nagid or the Rambam. Rather, the model of polysystems allows us to see that different signifying systems that occur within culture interpenetrate one another in expectable (and, to a certain extent, predictable) ways. Specifically, this condition obtains under the particular situation of diaspora, which, once again, I am designating as the cultural situation of a collective that is located in its own local culture and in the culture shared with another collective elsewhere. This is true, whether the practitioners of the culture are its great figures, as in these two examples, or whether they are lesser or even insignificant figures.

In her book *Models and Contacts: Arabic Literature and Its Impact on Medieval Jewish Culture*, Rina Drory elaborated this theoretical model with respect to the culture of which I speak. As she remarks with respect to what is usually called "borrowing": "Apparent borrowing may well conceal an entire network of transformations of the borrowed element, as demonstrated by Dunaš Ben Labraṭ's introduction of syllabic metre into Hebrew poetry in tenth-century Andalus. Contrary to the accepted view that Dunaš Ben Labraṭ adopted Arabic metre in its entirety, I contend that he only adopted its structural[24] principle, . . . adjusting it to Hebrew morphology."[25]

In a brilliant demonstration, Drory overturns a century's worth of scholarship that had argued that Dunaš utilized rather awkward phonological equivalents in Hebrew for the long and short vowels of Arabic, since Hebrew did not have vowel length as a phoneme.[26] First, she shows that Arabic meter is not based on the alternation of long and short syllables but rather on a much more complex opposition between different types of metrical units that are not identical with or coextensive with phonological units.[27] Although the account is a bit technical, it is nonetheless illuminating. Drory demonstrates that the Arabic meter is based on the alternation of two types of metrical units, one that is complex and one that is simplex. Dunaš found in Hebrew an equivalent in the alternation of complexes of schewa and a vowel versus units of a vowel alone. He gave these two types of units Hebrew equivalents (calques) of the Arabic terminology despite the fact that entirely different phonological entities were being mobilized in the two languages. The function is the same; the material elements producing that function are distinct in the two linguistic systems. Far from the rather passive-sounding "borrowing" or "influence," we have the active adaptation of a function from one linguistic system (Arabic) to another (Hebrew), realized by different means within each system. Drory writes: "The Spanish course of contacts is characterized by the 'invention' of new items for the functions borrowed from Arabic, as in the case of Dunaš's metre, and, in fact, as seen in the entire Spanish phenomena [*sic*] of constructing new poetic models for secular poetry."[28]

We find the same kind of active adaptation—and not slavish borrowing or passive influence—in Kanpanton's theory and practice of talmudic study in the Jewish Iberia of five hundred years later. The continuation of this cultural pattern by the later Iberian Jews—indeed, its elaboration into areas of cultural practice that, to the best of our knowledge, had not been developed by earlier Spanish Jews—should be considered as a survival of the particular diasporic polysystemic structure in which the Jews participated in Spain. By incorporating their talmudic study into that Arab Jewish polysystem, the structure of diaspora as the mobilization of a local and a trans-local cultural system at the same time becomes complete. An excellent example of the virtue of this approach comes in analyzing, once more, a point from the work of R"Y Kanpanton.

The Polysystem and the Logic of Talmud

In *Darkhe hatalmud*, Kanpanton writes: "In the beginning [of your study,] read the language two or three times with a joyful heart and a loud voice. Afterward, go back and study that language in depth, and take into your hand the simple meaning of that language and then go back and study again in depth that which is understood from the language and those words by implicature. The first is called the simple meaning, and the second is called the *diyyuq* of the Mishna, and the logicians call the simple meaning premise and the *diyyuq* [they call] conclusion."[29]

This is, at first glance, a very strange statement. Kanpanton seems to be confusing two entirely different kinds of logic: the logic of conversational implicature that we have in the Talmud, in which inferences are drawn by closely analyzing what is implied or presupposed by the Mishna; and syllogistic logic, to which the terms "premise" and "conclusion" apply. On second thought, Kanpanton is making a brilliant analogy. He is saying that the place of the syllogism in Greco-Arabic (Aristotelian) logic is taken in the Talmud by the logic of implicature. Most of the sugyot of the Talmud begin with the citation of a statement from the Mishna and the drawing of an inference from it: "It says 'on the fourth day'; therefore, on the fifth day, the law does not apply." Just as for Dunaš, a function in Arabic meter is analogized to a similar function in Hebrew, albeit not by the same means, so for Kanpanton, the function of the syllogism in Aristotle is analogized to the function of conversational logic in the Talmud.

We see that the rabbi, at the very crepuscule of Sefardic culture in Iberia, is making almost the identical move that Dunaš had made at its aurora. He has not slavishly borrowed the terms "premise" and "conclusion" from Arabic logic, nor has he been passively influenced by Arabic or by Greek learning. He has taken knowledge of his own from within a local system of culture and learning in which he participates and adapted it successfully and creatively to a trans-local system of culture and learning in which he also participates. Through the contact between his philosophical learning, on the one hand, and his intensive and extensive erudition in Talmud, on the other, he has come to discover something about the Talmud and its discourse. Remarkably, what he discovered turns out to be of signal importance for even our contemporary analysis of Jewish culture(s): the polysystemic study of Yiddish language and literature as well, owing to the diasporic nature of talmudic discourse.

From Greek to Yiddish: The Sefarad-Ashkenaz Polysystem

Within the Ashkenazi cultural memory, the invention of the method of *pilpul* and *ḥilluqim* ("divisions," as it is called—significantly) is laid at the door of Rabbi Yaʿakov Pollack, rabbi of Prague and Kraków in the late fifteenth and early sixteenth centuries.[30] Dimitrovsky taught us that *pilpul* and *ḥilluq* are not synonymous terms, with the latter in Poland (this includes Prague) a kind of lengthy discourse on a passage of the Talmud that organizes all the difficulties with the passage under a certain rubric and then resolves all of them in one fell swoop, producing an extraordinary impression among the students of the yeshiva.[31] Dimitrovsky is right on target in his identification of the *ḥilluq* (and separation of it from the practice of drawing fine distinctions between passages with which it had been muddled previously). He makes clear that the Sefardim also had the term *ḥilluq*, even if they used it differently.[32] He provides two alternative explanations for the development of this form in Ashkenaz: either Rabbi Pollack invented it out of whole cloth; or the Ashkenazim received this term of art and the art itself from the Sefardim, who had it earlier.[33] Although Dimitrovsky leans toward the first option, in my opinion, however, the second is much more plausible for two reasons: the first explanation gives us no plausible etymology for the term; and it is much more likely that the same term functioning at the same time in two related communities (even if somewhat mutatis mutandis) has come from one to the other and not spontaneously generated in both. Since, as I have shown above, the term makes perfect sense in its Sefardi acceptation and application as part of an entire logical framework while in its Ashkenazi usage is lexically inexplicable,[34] it would seem that here, too, as with *sebara mibbaḥuẓ*, it was the Sefardic world with its Greco-Arabic logic and epistemology that gave rise to this mode of interpretation. The *ḥilluq* developed among the Sefardim out of their deep engagement with the methods of scholastic philosophy in both its Arabic and Latin guises and in which the method of diaeresis was such a major part that it formed the very matter of the lecture by the teacher in the late Spanish yeshiva and its successors.

Within the Sefardic *ʿiyyun*, a special method of study goes under the name *ḥaluqah*, "division."[35] This is a method of Talmud study that is entirely embedded in the scholastic world of philosophy and theology. It is well known that Plato used collection and division in his later dialogues and even considered this the true dialectic in them. A famous example can be found in the *Sophist*. The *ḥaluqah* yields a disjunctive proposition to the effect that something is either this or that. It is then possible to prove that it is this by proving that it is not that or to prove that it is that by proving that it is not this. This can be built into a whole series of such disjunctions that yields a classification as well as a demonstration of its truth. This method of reasoning, which was very well known by the Islamic logicians and much used by the theologians of the *kalam*, was very early adopted into Jewish cultural circles in Muslim lands.[36] Maimonides makes use of this style of reasoning explicitly, referring to it as *ḥaluqah*.[37] The standard terminology for this operation, which can be found explicitly in the Sefardi talmudic interpretation is, as it is in Maimonides: "It is inescapable [לא ימלט] that it must be one of the two possibilities." When expanded into a series of dichotomous divisions of an entire genus into species such that at every turn, only one of two possibilities is real, effective use of disproving the rejected alternatives (Arabic, *taqṣim*) provides proof of the accepted ones.[38] Since I have and will treat this topic at length elsewhere, all that is necessary for my argument here is this brief demonstration that there is a direct connection between the philosophical usage in Greek, the theological usage in Arabic *kalam*, and, finally, the usage in the talmudic interpretations of the Sefardim of the fifteenth century, where it developed elaborate forms that became the center of lectures in Rabbi Yitzḥak Kanpanton's yeshiva.

It seems that the reason that Dimitrovsky did not want to assert that the Ashkenazim learned this from the Sefardim is the differences in practice between the two schools.[39] The Ashkenazi *ḥilluq* is very different in structure, as we see from its preserved examples and descriptions gathered and analyzed by Dimitrovsky. This distinction makes less of a difference than seems at first glance. One of the most typical ways that a Sefardic *ḥaluqah* begins is with the technical philosophical term cited above, inter alia from Maimonides: "It is inescapable that one of the two following options must be correct, but," while Dimitrovsky has shown that in Ashkenaz, the *ḥilluq* most often began with a difficulty of the sort: "What can you say; it must be this or that, and there is a difficulty in both directions [מה נפשך]." In other words, we see the same logic and rhetoric at work in both, even though the Ashkenazim use more talmudic language and the Sefardim use the terminology of medieval scholasticism. It is this hybridization between the native talmudic terminology and the Aristotelian/scholastic philosophical one that marks the diasporic nature of such talmudic interpretation. I suggest that the answer to the puzzle created by the dilemma being the near-ubiquitous form of the opening statement of the *ḥilluq* can be found once more in the genealogy of that method of Ashkenazi *pilpul* from the *ḥaluqah* of the Sefardim, where, consonant with its original usage, it is the division into two exclusive possibilities that defines the form.[40] All these practices, the *sebara mibbaḥuẓ* (see appendix), the endless raising and demolishing of fallacies to demonstrate and understand truth, and the use of diaeresis, are thus intimately connected among the Sefardim with the entire epistemology of hermeneutics as derived from philosophical practice.

As I hope to have shown, the routes of this method of talmudic study are from Sefarad to Ashkenaz, probably in the fifteenth century, and perhaps earlier. If my reconstruction of this history is load-bearing, so to speak, it provides an elegant illustration for the productivity of diasporic cultures for which I argue. The movement of cultural goods that is enabled by the trans-local connections of the cultural actors and collectives involved makes for importantly creative developments. A mode of study of Talmud born in northern Europe in a world of intense textualism fostered by Christian and Jewish authors alike travels with Jewish travelers to another talmudic world, where they do things differently. This is much like the process by which, I have suggested, the Talmud came into being, in the fertile contact between Babylonia and Palestine. When these modes of study arrive in Sefarad, they transform talmudic learning but are further transformed by contact with the deep, rich, and long contacts that those Jews had enjoyed with Greek intellectual culture as it appeared in Arabic. Now it returns to Ashkenaz, having undergone a sea change and fructifying the modes of learning there, revivifying them with enough new energy to keep them going for two centuries or more.

It wasn't only to Ashkenaz that Sefardic learning traveled, for it also, radiating from Spain, it gave rise to the great talmudic cultures of the Ottoman Empire and North Africa. The methods of study developed by R"Y Kanpanton, his predecessors, and successors became the method of study of the Talmud in all the Sefardic world, especially after 1492. There may be no question that the expulsion from Spain, like others before and after, was painful, exceedingly and in may ways, to the expelled Jews, but it was not traumatic. These Jews simply went about their business of taking their traveling homeland with them and rebuilding it in new (mostly Muslim) homes. Among the places where this learning was transplanted are Adrianople, Nicopole, Constantinople, Fez, and, especially, Safed in the Galilee.[41]

Here my story comes full circle. The learning of Talmud, which began in the Galilee at the beginning of the first millennium or so, had returned now in the form of the great yeshiva founded there by Rabbi Yitzḥak Berav, one of the greatest of Kanpanton's disciples. In this distant outpost of the Ottoman Empire was one of the greatest centers of Jewish learning in the sixteenth century, but the center was an integral part of the framework and network of the communities of learning that had radiated from the yeshiva of R"Y Kanpanton in Zamora (Castile), and these communities carried the yeshiva's Greco-Arabic talmudic hermeneutics with them. The scholars of these great yeshiva communities traveled back and forth; for example, some lived for a while in Turkish yeshiva centers, for a while in Fez, and on to Cairo, Sofia, and thence to Safed.[42] It is not inapposite, nor is it entirely new, to refer to this network of talmudic scholarship and culture as yet another new Jewish diaspora. Spain is the point of origin, but what makes this a diaspora, in my interpretation, are these constant cultural interconnections among the various new and renewed settlements. The Talmud had come back to Palestine, but Palestine was now in (a) diaspora.

Frequently, perhaps most frequently, when we think of Safed in the sixteenth century, it is the mysticism that comes to mind, for this mountain fastness of Torah was arguably the major center of kabbalistic creativity at that time. However, under the leadership of R"Y Kanpanton's great disciple Rabbi Yaʿakov Berav, the Sefardic tradition of close logical talmudic study was carried on here, too.[43] Berav justly considered himself the direct continuation of the Torah study of Kanpanton, the last Castilian master.[44]

To communicate most effectively how influential this community was, I mention that Rabbi Yosef Karo, author of the definitive code of Torah law, the *Shulḥan Arukh*, was a student of R"Y Berav in that yeshiva, and his own Talmud study followed the modes of analysis developed by the latter's teacher, Rabbi Kanpanton. Outpost of the Ottoman Empire it may have been, but Galilee had again become a center of Torah, bringing the round full circle. Now the dual cultural location, paradoxically, was the Galilee as the local culture and the entire Sefardic world (and, as we shall see, Ashkenaz as well) as the trans-local culture. As my teacher concludes his discussion: "The modes of study and the systems that were established in the yeshiva of R"Y Berav in Safed set the patterns for the yeshivot that were set up by his students and the students of his students, and their influence was felt in them for many a year"[45]—and not only, of course, in the Sefardic world.

Beginning in the sixteenth century, the rabbis of Ashkenaz and Eastern Europe were transfixed once again by the style of learning, by the methods of *ʿiyyun* that had developed in Sefarad.[46] One of the most influential of all rabbinic works, the halakhic and spiritual *Shnei Luḥot Habrit*, of Rabbi Yeshaya Horowitz, seeks to reform decadent Ashkenazi *pilpul* by introducing the much more sober and logical methods of the Sefardim. Toward the end of his life, its author comes to Safed. He copied Kanpanton's work, word for word, in his book (attributed, of course), to promote learning by that method in Poland and environs. As Dimitrovsky argued, he came for the kabbalah, but judging again from his masterpiece, which became central to the learning and spirituality all over the Jewish world in the seventeenth century and until today, it was not only for the kabbalah that he stayed. He, along with others, contributed to the great efflorescence of Ashkenazic learning in the style of the Sefardic *ʿiyyun*.[47]

My only variance from Dimitrovsky's reconstruction of this moment is that while he writes, "in truth, this was nothing but the way of Ashkenazi *pilpul* in its original form and purity,"[48] I would write something like, "in truth, this was nothing but a return to the original Sefardic *pilpul* that had originally spawned that of the Ashkenazim." The point about diaspora has been made, either way. We find here, too, the absolute justice of Prof. Dimitrovsky's declaration, quoted in Chapter 1 of this book: "The period from the beginning of the eleventh century and until the time when the world of Talmud ceased to be the world of the Jewish people . . . in its content, its spirit, and its tendencies, is a period in which the Talmud is the center of the world of the Jew."[49] But, as we have seen, wherever Jews lived, that very center, the Talmud, was inflected by contact with a local culture as well.

If my interpretation is right, it is virtually certain that this method was developed in the epistemological context within which the Arabic terms, translated from the Greek, flourished—namely, al-Andalus—and came from there into Ashkenaz, even as early as the fifteenth century.[50] That is how diaspora works. What is produced within one local cultural context moves to another via the transcultural connections and then adds to cultural practice, where it becomes transformed in the new cultural environment as well and then travels farther. This is how a homeland travels.

The Way of Shas: Yiddish and Women's Diaspora

> What would it mean to theorize a feminist articulation of diaspora?[51]

In his discussion of the work of the Boyarins on diaspora published in the early 1990s,[52] James Clifford rightly took us to task for not considering the question of gender and its differential impact in the social structures of diasporic societies and in the theorization of diaspora. We subsequently attempted to answer at least some of the questions raised by Clifford, as well as other critics of our work, and of the concept of diaspora.[53] The critiques of the concept of diaspora from feminists go on.[54] Clifford essentially made this point, when he wrote: "When diasporic experience is viewed in terms of displacement rather than placement, traveling, rather than dwelling, and disarticulation rather than articulation, then the experiences of men will tend to predominate."[55] I would rephrase Clifford's remark to read: When diasporic experience is defined as the product of synchronic connection occasioned by shared cultural practice, the experiences of men will tend to predominate, women frequently having been excluded from the very traveling cultural practices (and the travel) that define and sustain the diaspora. The medieval narrative that served as the launching point for this book is an unabashed illustration of this theme.

The double erasure of women in this text, implicit in the case of Rabbi Ḥushiel, who marries and begets in Kairawan without a woman being mentioned, and explicit in the case of Moses, who loses his wife but arrives with his son in Cordova, signifies something else. The disembedding of these rabbis from families of their origin marks even more strongly the newness of this new diaspora. As "founding fathers," they must, for the purpose of the story and the legend, be seen as generating entirely in the new place, of themselves. It would seem, nonetheless, that the explicit notation of the fact that Rabbi Moses's wife spoke in Hebrew might suggest an answer to the question of whether Jewish women could have a diaspora, seeing that they were excluded from the Republic of Talmudic Letters. The fact that Ibn Daud explicitly remarks that she spoke Hebrew with her husband in this context is an indicator of two things: that they had a "secret" language, a language that the oppressor wouldn't understand; and, even more important in this context, that the language that she knew as well would bind him *and her* with other Jewish folk from other places, hence a diasporic tongue. Traditional Jewish life has suppressed female autonomy and creativity nearly entirely. Nonetheless, in a theoretical account of diaspora, it would be misleading, I think, to say that Jewish women were not part of one, an erasure on top of an erasure.

As Clifford has also pointed out: "Retaining focus on specific histories of displacement and dwelling keeps the ambivalent politics of diaspora in view. Women's experiences are particularly revealing. Do diaspora experiences reinforce or loosen gender subordination? On the one hand, maintaining connections with homelands, with kinship networks, and with religious and cultural traditions may renew patriarchal structures. On the other, new roles and demands, new political spaces, are opened up by diaspora interactions."[56]

In this closing discussion, I hope to give a very partial example of such a focus, as called for by Clifford. I offer first a very important articulation from Clifford: "It need not detract unduly from its force to ask whether Rabbi Saʿadya's disaggregated identity would have been restricted, or differently routed, if he were a woman. How did women 'mix' cultures? And how have they transmitted, 'genealogically,' the marks and messages of tradition? How have women embodied diasporic Judaism, and how has Judaism marked, empowered, or constrained their bodies?"[57] Without attempting to show the way to a complete answer to these questions—which must be asked—I suggest a partial (in every sense) response to some of them. At least one key is the question of language. The example of Yiddish, functioning something like the Hebrew of our medieval narrative, perhaps provides one approach.

As the Jews moved with their talmudic culture into Slavic territories, Yiddish was the vehicle through which the language of the Talmud became the daily shared language of what was then the largest part of Jewry.[58] Naomi Seidman has demonstrated to what extent Yiddish was figured as the "women's language," as opposed to the masculine Hebrew.[59] But Yiddish was also the language of *lernen*, of the study of Talmud in the yeshiva, and the everyday language that these Jews spoke with one another and with their wives. I am suggesting that Yiddish itself became the vehicle for a diaspora shared by men and women, one that was a product of the culture of Talmud study that constituted this diaspora, as I have been arguing throughout. It was this new sensibility of the Talmud as the language of Jewish discourse and life that gave rise to the particular Jewish culture later called "The Talmud's Way," the whole culture in which the Talmud was the air that Jews breathed and the water that they drank (as well as the milk delivered by Tevye, Shalom Aleikhem's archetypical Yiddish-speaking proletarian whose own language is rife with talmudic allusions).

The capacity for the production of the Way of the Talmud is located by Max Weinreich in that same condition of the Babylonian Talmud in which I have been locating the repeated formation of diasporas with a talmudic homeland: "This is truly the Way of the Shas," that is, of Talmud. "The very language of the holy Gemara [Talmud] came originally to the Jews from the outside, together with a wealth of other culture patterns that came from the Persians, Babylonians, Greeks, and Romans."[60] In other words, it was the particular and originary hybridism of the Talmud's language that enabled it to be the vehicle of repeatedly new Jewish hybridisms.

Why does the great historian of the Yiddish language, Max Weinreich, refer to Ashkenazi Jewish life as it developed from the Middle Ages in the Rhineland up to and including the Eastern European Jewish communities of prewar modernity as "The Way of the Talmud"? As he points out, that collocation, in its original sense, did not mean what he wants to say. Originally, as used by Rashi and other talmudic interpreters, the expression means simply the pattern, the mode of the Talmud's discourse, something internal to the book. Weinreich brilliantly adapts it to mean the way of a culture and a language that has made that book its total *Weltanschauung*, and for whom the Way of the Talmud has become a way of life:[61] "Ashkenazic Jewishness, the Way of the Shas, is a view of life and a way of life; incorporated in this system are the designations for human relations and actions. . . . It may be said that Jewishness becomes religion only with the arrival of the Emancipation. . . . But up to the Emancipation, Ashkenaz did not operate in terms of religion *and* world; the culture system of Jewishness *was* world. Until to today we see the reflection of Jewishness in the Yiddish language."[62]

Weinreich cites many examples, lovely and homely, of the ways that the Talmud inspirited the daily and everyday language of Yiddish speakers. Thus, the humble "ladybug" becomes in Yiddish *Moyshe Rabeyne's kiele*, "the little cow of our Rabbi, Moses." As Weinreich emphasizes, a usage like this ties the speakers of Yiddish, male and female, to the whole "vertical" tradition of Jewish life and discourse, especially in the designation of Moses as "Moyshe Rabeyne" from the talmudic Hebrew "Moshe Rabbenu," our Rabbi, Moses.[63] I can go a bit further than Weinreich did in exploring this term. This is a precise example of my notion of diaspora, since, in other German dialects, this beetle is called *Marienkälbchen*, the "little calf of Mary." The little bug has been converted from the calf of Our Lady to the little cow of Our Rabbi via a talmudic ecotypification; more precisely (in truth, who knows who took from whom, and who cares?), a shared positive religious association between Jews and Christians with this harmless, pretty little beetle has been translated into Jewish and Christian German dialects, respectively. Such is the diasporic Talmud's Way.

In the earlier examples and periods, my focus has been more on the local as interaction between Jewish and non-Jewish (always male) intellectual elites; in early modern Ashkenaz, the element of the local is generated by the intense interaction with everyday speech, which is connected to and separated from the speech of the surrounding populace. This is a good way to make the case that the modes of diaspora that I am projecting here are not exclusively elite or exclusively male.[64] However, we must not make the common and popular mistake of assuming that Eastern European Jewish intellectual elites were not an integral part of the intellectual world around them, as earlier ones had been: in his recent book, *The Genius*, Eliyahu Stern has eloquently shown how embedded a figure such as Eliyahu of Vilna, the doyen of traditional talmudic study in the eighteenth century, was in the currents of thought that flowed then through Central Europe, including those of figures such as Leibniz and his disciples and how much his classical talmudic scholarship was of a piece with them.[65] Once again, the so-called influence does not run in only one direction, since Leibniz was importantly informed by kabbalah and by Maimonides' *Guide*, for the Latin translation of which he wrote a preface.[66]

Talmudic discourse infuses the very ways of thinking of Yiddish speakers. "Studying" had such a different function in Jewish culture as compared with its role in general European cultures. In the latter, it was primarily a matter for a certain elite, and in many circles a not particularly prestigious elite; in the Way of the Talmud, studying Talmud was the most ubiquitous cultural practice and the most prestigious, and it was for everyone, in some way or another.[67]

I am not denying that there was severe hierarchy within these societies or forgetting the ways that the culture of learning was exclusionary; nonetheless, this culture of *lernen* suffused the entire system of Jewish cultures via the Jewish languages and their respective encodings of the Way of the Talmud such that everyday speech for everyone was brought into it. Nonetheless, in the heyday of the Talmud's Way, everyone who spoke Yiddish, men and women, was part of the Way of the Talmud, perhaps most when they spoke of so-called secular matters.

Excursus: Apocryphal Truths

An outstanding method of talmudic interpretation developed by Yitzḥak Kanpanton was known as *sebara mibbaḥuẓ* (lit., "opinion from outside"), which I will translate here, for reasons that will become apparent, "understanding by subaudition." The routes of this method of interpretation are an example of what I mean by diasporic cultural practice. Here is the rabbi's description of the force of this technique: "Diligently investigate in any utterance or sentence what you would have thought from your own reasoning or understood from your intelligence before the tanna or the amora intervened. For you will have a great benefit from this—namely, if you would have understood of your own as he does, then you can ask of him what he has come to communicate to us. On the other hand, if your own reasoning is opposed to his, you must investigate to find what forced him to say what he did and what the weakness is or fallacy in what you had thought. And this is what is called *sebara mibbaḥuẓ*."[68]

The *sebara mibbaḥuẓ* is what would have been understood by the commentator from the language of the Torah or of the Mishna without the necessity for an interpretive intervention on the part of the tannaim or amoraim. The origin of the term is not totally established. I propose that the *sebara mibbaḥuẓ* is a calque on an Arabic logical term, ultimately going back to a Greek term in the commentaries on Aristotle. In that literature, we find the Greek term εζωθεν in the sense of what is not expressed explicitly in language because it is understood by the intelligence of the hearer or reader without need for it to be expressed. So we find it used in Ammonius's commentary on Aristotle: "What is required in a modal proposition is not merely a verb which includes the copula, but the copula itself, either explicit or supplied to the proposition from outside by subaudition [εξωθεν τη προτασει υπακονομενου], for we say: either 'It is possible that Socrates will go,' or 'It is possible that Socrates will be a musician' with the copula expressed. But we can also express these propositions without the copula thus: 'Possible that Socrates will go.' We hold that in the latter case, the copula is understood [Ammonius 223, 30-224, 10]."[69]

We find that Ammonius uses the term "from outside" to refer to a linguistic sign that does not need to be expressed in the language for the sentence to be understood but can be supplied from the mind.[70] It is not difficult to imagine a talmudic thinker inquiring why it is ever used if it need not be. An even more exact correspondence to our usage is found in Al-Farabi, who frequently uses the expression *aḍmarahu wa-fahimahu min khārij*. As Farabi's editor, F. W. Zimmerman, remarks, "*min khārij* presumably is an exegetical concept, and as such occurs in a set phrase literally rendering the Greek in the glosses of the Baghdad Organon."[71] As Zimmerman further explains: "The expression *aḍmarahu wa-fahimahu min khārij* [to supply in the mind and understand it from the outside] doubly translates (first idiomatically, then literally) εξωθεν τη προτασει υπακονομενου, an expression frequently found . . . in the Greek commentaries."[72]

In short, the Greek ἔξωθεν calqued by the Arabic *min khārij* provides an exact source for Kanpanton's uses of *mibbaḥuẓ*. The correspondence is even more exact in the case of interpreting a commentator, such as Rashi; for then, the question is, Given that I would have understood a certain point *mibbaḥuẓ* because it is implied in the language, why did Rashi have to tell it to me explicitly? It is most significant and interesting to see that the term, once appropriated, takes on a life of its own and develops several variant meanings, among them some that are central and ubiquitous in Ashkenazi *pilpul* as well.[73] As Dimitrovsky demonstrates, the *sebara mibbaḥuẓ* is the most ubiquitous, constant, and well-attested term and concept of both Sefardi and Ashkenazi *pilpul*.

Notes

PRELUDE

1. Edward W. Said, *Reflections on Exile and Other Essays*, Convergences (Cambridge, Mass.: Harvard University Press, 2000) 177.

2. Khachig Tölölyan, "Rethinking Diaspora(s): Stateless Power in the Transnational Moment," *Diaspora* 5.1 (1996): 30.

3. Which is certainly very old, if not originary. See Willem Cornelis van Unnik, *Das Selbstverständnis der jüdischen Diaspora in der hellenistisch-römischen Zeit*, Arbeiten zur Geschichte des antiken Judentums und des Urchristentums (Leiden: Brill, 1993) 76–78.

4. For these three points as definitive for the late ancient usages of the term, esp. in the Church Fathers: "3) Er wird immer in Zusammenhang mit den Juden gebraucht, die, aus ihrem Heimatland vertrieben, in der Diaspora leben; 4) dabei ist Diaspora entweder der Aktion des Zerstreuens oder geographisch die Lage des Zerstreutseins; 5) das Leben der Juden in der Diaspora wird im allgemeinen ungünstig als Strafe beurteilt" (ibid., 79).

5. Robin Cohen, *Global Diasporas: An Introduction*, 2nd ed. (London: Routledge, 2008) 1. Note well that Cohen writes, only a page later, "As I shall argue in Chapter 2, the catastrophic origins of the Jewish diaspora have been unduly emphasized in their collective consciousness" (ibid., 2), to which my response would be that different groups of Jews have had different collective consciousnesses at different times and places and in the same time and place as well.

6. For a similar move with respect to "folklore," cf. Dina Stein, "Let the 'People' Go: On the 'Folk' and Their 'Lore' as Tropes in the Reconstruction of Rabbinic Culture," *Prooftexts* 29 (2009): 206–41.

7. R. Cohen, 7.

8. Ibid., 8.

9. Citations from ibid., 10–11.

10. See Jonathan Boyarin, in Jonathan Boyarin and Daniel Boyarin, *Powers of Diaspora: Two Essays on the Relevance of Jewish Culture* (Minneapolis: University of Minnesota Press, 2002) 11.

11. R. Cohen, 2.

12. For the distinction, see A. von Selms in RGG II 175, s.v. "diaspora." Discussion at Unnik, 64.

13. Unnik, 68.

14. For the nonequivalence of Greek *diaspora* and Hebrew גולה, see ibid., 82–83. Unnik makes the excellent observation that the Septuagint, in its usage of "diaspora," draws together several different Hebrew words and thus creates a new technical term, a new concept in Greek: "Sie haben damit die Lage ihres Volkes als etwas anderes als eine 'Gefangenschaft,' ein 'Exil' oder eine 'Deportation' u.s.w. charakterisiert, Begriffe, die *auch* in der griechischen Geschichte und Sprache bekannt waren" (ibid., 85).

15. Ibid., 85 (translation mine).

16. Ibid., 87.

17.

משנה מסכת אבות פרק ד

משנה יד: רבי נהוראי אומר הוי גולה למקום תורה ואל תאמר שהיא תבוא אחריך שחביריך יקיימוה בידך ואל בינתך אל תשען:

18. Steve Mason, "Our Language and Theirs: Categories and Identities" (unpublished essay, 2013). Referring to Philo, *Legat.* 203, 281; *Flacc.* 46. Cf. Strabo 4.1.4; 10.4.17.

19. Stefan Helmreich, "Kinship, Nation, and Paul Gilroy's Concept of Diaspora," *Diaspora* 2.2 (1992): 245.

20. Martin Baumann, "Diaspora: Genealogies of Semantics and Transcultural Comparison," *Numen* 47.3 (2000): 313–37.

21. For important discussion, see Johannes Tromp, "The Ancient Jewish Diaspora: Some Linguistic and Sociological Observations," *Strangers and Sojourners: Religious Communities in the Diaspora*, ed. Gerrie ter Haar (Leuven: Peeters, 1998) 15–16.

22. Ibid., 17–18.

CHAPTER 1

1. Tölölyan, 3.

2. The list of scholars who have treated it is provided in Gerson D. Cohen, "The Story of the Four Captives," *Proceedings of the American Academy for Jewish Research* 29 (1960–61): 70, which reads like a Who's Who of the Wissenschaft des

Judentums. As Cohen remarks, most of this scholarship was an attempt to figure out what "really happened."

3. A more recent Hebrew study of this text has been produced in Sarah Tsefatman, *Rosh ve-Rishon: Yisud Manhigut be-Sifrut Yisra'el* (Jerusalem: Magnes, 2010) 83–99, to which I shall refer below as appropriate.

4. "There is weighty evidence that the Franco-German legend on the three helmless ships antedates Ibn Daud's story by at least a century. As Hans Lewy noted in quite another connection, the motif of Jews being put to sea in three ships by Titus (or Vespasian) goes back to early Rabbinic accounts of the destruction of the Temple, specifically to Abot de R. Nathan, where it is told that Titus dismantled the sacred vessels of the Temple 'and filled three ships with men, women and children in order to boast of his triumph abroad.' Hence, the theme of three ships filled with captive Jews is an ancient one, probably of Tannaitic origin. . . . For his story of the four captives, Ibn Daud drew on an old recension of the legend telling of Vespasian's deportation of Jews by ship." G. Cohen, "The Story of the Four Captives," 77, 84. Tsefatman argues that the story is a virtual anthology of three individual founding stories, of which the Cordova one is of most interest to Ibn Daud (Tsefatman, 85–86), which seems plausible and also somewhat misses the point. I wonder also at the plausibility of Tsefatman's assumption that each of the communities had a founding legend of the same structure, captive rabbi, redemption, and revelation of identity, which could then be gathered by Ibn Daud into his "anthology," as she calls it. Although I am no scholar of folk narrative, I question, on the terms of that discipline as far as I know them, the procedure whereby a whole narrative for each of these scholars is reconstructed on the basis of some rules or other and then claimed to have been abridged.

5. G. Cohen, "The Story of the Four Captives," 91–93. This sentence is spread over three pages owing to its footnotes, which is indicative of the amount of erudition and important argumentation packed into the notes of that work.

6. For the story, Gerson D. Cohen, *A Critical Edition with a Translation and Notes of the Book of Tradition (Sefer ha-Qabbalah) by Abraham Ibn Daud*, Judaica Texts and Translations 3 (Philadelphia: Jewish Publication Society of America, 1967) 63–67.

7. The historical story is more complex than this. David M. Goodblatt, *Rabbinic Instruction in Sasanian Babylonia*, Studies in Judaism in Late Antiquity 9 (Leiden: E. J. Brill, 1975), demonstrated several decades ago that the academies were founded quite a bit later than the legends suppose and that earlier rabbinic instruction had been pursued in small study circles around individual teacher-Rabbis. By the time of which we are speaking, the great yeshivot had been in existence for centuries. See also Isaiah M. Gafni, "The Babylonian Yeshiva as Reflected in Bava Kama 111a," *Tarbiẓ* 49 (1980): 292–301, in Hebrew; English summary, v–vi.

8. G. Cohen, "The Story of the Four Captives," 59 n. 9.

9. The interpretation of the story will be only slightly damaged if we render הכנסת כלה in its more usual sense of "going to a wedding," although the punch of the irony will surely be weakened. For more on the failure of the support of the Babylonian yeshivot from Spain, see Shraga Abramson, *Ba-Merkazim uvatefutsot bi-Tekufat ha-Ge'onim* (Jerusalem: Mosad Harav Kook, 1965) 84–85. Writing of the exactly contemporaneous Italian chronicle, *The Scroll of Aḥima'az*, Robert Bonfil wonders why it does not mention the well-known connections between the Italian centers of talmudic learning and the Babylonian academies and answers that this is a dramatic demonstration of the independence of that Italian center from the East and its establishment of itself as a new center (Robert Bonfil, "Myth, Rhetoric, History? A Study in the Chronicle of Aḥima'az," in Hebrew, *Culture and Society in Medieval Jewry*, ed. Reuven Bonfil, Menahem Ben-Sasson, and Yosef Hacker [Jerusalem: Merkaz Zalman Shazar le-Toldot Yisrael, 1989] 102–3). See also his very brief discussion of our four captives (Bonfil, "Myth, Rhetoric, History," 115).

10. Robert Bonfil, *History and Folklore in a Medieval Jewish Chronicle: The Family Chronicle of Aḥima'az ben Paltiel* (Leiden: Brill, 2009) 48.

11. See, with Cohen, Arabic *madrasa*. Cohen, "college synagogue" for Hebrew כנסת המדרש. Cohen's translation is, of course, entirely accurate but less than clear here.

12. Cohen, "conducted a school and interpreted [the traditions] more or less [accurately]," for the Hebrew היו עושים מדרש ומפרשים ועולים ויורדים (lit., "were conducting a school and interpreting going up and going down") is an impossible translation, as are all the earlier ones that he cites at G. Cohen, "The Story of the Four Captives," 61 n. 22. My translation, also doubtful, is based on the talmudic idiom בהא נחתינן ובהא סלקינן, "We are constantly busy with this" (lit., "in this, we are descending and ascending), as found at Pesaḥim 87b. While this translation is by no means certain, it has the virtue of being relatively neutral vis-à-vis the meaning of the text. For a similar idiom in Greek, see Πυθαγόρας δέ, τοιαῦτα μοχθήσας περὶ θεῶν καὶ τὴν ἄνω κάτω πορείαν ποιησάμενος (Theophilus of Antioch, *Ad Autolycum*, ed. and trans. Robert M. Grant, Oxford Early Christian Texts [Oxford: Clarendon, 1970] 106). "Going up and down" here seems to be an intensification of making great efforts. Another possibility is that "going up" and "going down" mean refuting and defending, for which see Adiel Schremer, "'He Posed Him a Difficulty and Placed Him': A Study in the Evolution of the Text of TB Bava Kama 117a," *Tarbiẓ* 66.3 (April–June 1997): 403–15, in Hebrew; English summary, viii.

13. G. Cohen, *A Critical Edition with a Translation and Notes of the Book of Tradition (Sefer ha-Qabbalah) by Abraham Ibn Daud*, 65–66. For the Umayyad king, it was advantageous to have his Jewish subjects not dependent on authority in

the rival Abbasid Empire (Talya Fishman, *Becoming the People of the Talmud: Oral Torah as Written Tradition in Medieval Jewish Cultures*, Jewish Culture and Contexts [Philadelphia: University of Pennsylvania Press, 2011] 77).

14. Tsefatman's main contribution is to show the persistence of this form of narrative from rabbinic to medieval Jewish times.

15. That it is of no practical matter does not mean that it is devoid of cultural significance. See Naftali S. Cohn, *The Memory of the Temple and the Making of the Rabbis*, Divinations: Rereading Late Ancient Religion (Philadelphia: University of Pennsylvania Press, 2013).

16. G. Cohen, "The Story of the Four Captives," 93.

17. Ibid., 113.

18. "In discussing Safran's constitution of a comparative field, I worried about the extent to which diaspora, defined as dispersal, presupposed a center. If this center becomes associated with an actual 'national' territory—rather than with a reinvented 'tradition,' a 'book,' a portable eschatology—it may devalue what I called the lateral axes of diaspora" (James Clifford, "Diasporas," *Cultural Anthropology* 9 [August 1994]: 323).

19. See, too, on a related point, Fishman, 28.

20. For this passage from Rav Hai Gaon, see ibid., 49–51.

21. Hayyim Zalman Dimitrovsky, "Do the Jews Have a Middle Ages?," *Meḥkarim be-Mada'e ha-Yahadut*, ed. Moshe Bar Asher (Jerusalem: Hebrew University, 1986) 265, in Hebrew.

22. G. Cohen, "The Story of the Four Captives," 94.

23. See discussion and sources apud Bonfil, "Myth, Rhetoric, History," 102–3. Where Bonfil interprets these phenomena under the sign of *translatio scientiae*, I wish to read into them greater significance for the interpretation of Jewish diaspora as constantly forming and reforming and thus for the theory of diaspora *simpliciter*. Cf. also ibid., 106.

24. For this text, see Avraham Grossman, "The Yeshiva of Eretz Israel: The Literary Output and the Relationship with the Diaspora," *The History of Jerusalem: The Early Muslim Period, 638–1099*, ed. Joshua Prawer and Haggai Ben-Shammai (Jerusalem: Yad Izḥak Ben-Zvi, 1996) 246–47. It is fascinating that while Grossman marks the importance of this text in several ways, he misses the point that it represents the defeat of the Babylonian training "in the yeshiva of Hai Gaon" by the Kairawani Rabbenu Ḥananel and his colleague Rav Nissim Gaon of that same city. This is an important and very marked moment, given that Kairawan is the very model of a place that relied on the written text of the Talmud exclusively, the target of Rav Sherira Gaon's highly charged plea to them to remain within the fold of geonic hegemony (see, inter alia, Fishman, 29, on this point). This is surely connected

with the production of the first great sustained written commentaries on the Talmud as well, by these two Kairawani rabbis.

25. The innovative thoughts about diaspora emerging from the theoretical literature do not support the view (held by some such theoreticians) that "the" Jewish diaspora—ironically—is exceptional in the history of diasporas. In contrast, I would assert that the new approaches can be supported and deepened from analysis of Jewish diaspora—or set of diasporas.

26. In its original usage by Rabbenu Tam, this "Torah" referred not to the Babylonian Talmud as carried by our four captives but to the Palestinian liturgical traditions that had held sway in Byzantine Italy. For discussion, see Bonfil, "Myth, Rhetoric, History," 106–7. My use of this bon mot is thus something of an appropriation in its own right.

27. See excellent discussion by Unnik, 65.

28. I thus disagree slightly in emphasis with Bonfil, who argues that the Babylonian "contents" become simply a resource among others for these Italian and then Spanish Jews (Bonfil, "Myth, Rhetoric, History," 105). They do not need Babylonia any more, but the Babylonian Talmud remains the center, with other texts arrayed around it like ancillae.

29. This trope has, of course, been mobilized before by Jewish writers, from Heinrich Heine through George Steiner, and now to Simon Schama. Each has used it differently, and I, too, am using it in quite a different (although not necessarily incompatible) fashion.

30. See Rogers Brubaker, "The 'Diaspora' Diaspora," *Ethnic and Racial Studies* 28.1 (2005): 1–19; and, esp., Martin Sökefeld, "Mobilizing in Transnational Space: A Social Movement Approach to the Formation of Diaspora," *Global Networks* 6.3 (2006): 265–84.

31. Baumann, 322.

32. Brent Hayes Edwards, "The Uses of Diaspora," *Social Text* 19.1 (spring 2001): 45.

33. W. E. B. (William Edward Burghardt) Du Bois, *The World and Africa: An Inquiry into the Part Which Africa Has Played in World History* (New York: International, 1965) 7.

34. E.g., William Safran, "Diasporas in Modern Societies: Myths of Homeland and Return," *Diaspora* 1 (1991): 83–99.

35. R. Cohen, 7 (emphasis original).

36. This answers the complaints of some social scientists to the effect that diaspora has become so commonly used that it is a meaningless taxon; it also answers the rejection of diaspora as overly concerned with an essentialized place. The reasons to reject diachronic considerations for "lateral connections" can be exemplified via the

following quotation: "The highly motivated Koreans and Vietnamese toiling hard to become prosperous in bustling Los Angeles, the haggard Palestinians living in dreary refugee camps near Beirut and Amman, the beleaguered Turks dwelling in cramped apartments in Berlin, and the frustrated Russians in Estonia, all have much in common. All of them, along with Indians, Chinese, Japanese, Africans, African-Americans, Jews, Palestinians, Greeks, Gypsies, Romanians, Poles, Kurds, Armenians and numerous other groups permanently residing outside of their countries of origin, but maintaining contacts with people back in their old homelands, are members of ethno-national diasporas" (Gabriel Scheffer, *Diaspora Politics: At Home Abroad* [Cambridge: Cambridge University Press, 2003] 1). There is no sense in which it could be said of historical Jews that they were "maintaining contacts with people back in their old homelands"; the cultural contacts that they were maintaining were with other Jews and had nothing to do with an "old homeland." It is not clear in which sense Palestine remained even a country of origin. Indeed, the constitution of the modern invented homeland called the State of Israel could easily be seen as the product of migration of Jews from several homelands.

37. Finbarr B. Flood, *Objects of Translation: Material Culture and Medieval "Hindu-Muslim" Encounter* (Princeton, N.J.: Princeton University Press, 2009) 1. I am grateful to my Wissenschaftskolleg colleague Elizabeth Key Fowden, who pointed out the importance of this book to me.

38. See, e.g., Rina Drory, *Models and Contacts: Arabic Literature and Its Impact on Medieval Jewish Culture*, Brill's Series in Jewish Studies 25 (Leiden: Brill, 2000) 184, citing the tenth-century Rabbi Saʿadya Gaon.

39. See, on this, Unnik, 53. See also ibid., 62.

40. Cf. Isaiah M. Gafni, *Land, Center and Diaspora: Jewish Constructs in Late Antiquity* (Sheffield: Sheffield Academic Press, 1997) 53–57. Note how this way of thinking renders "double consciousness" a highly specific, historical empirical notion and not simply another name for postmodernist dissemination. While coming closest to my approach, Baumann still underplays the doubleness of the cultural orientation, to both the local and the trans-local, when he writes:

> The definition places emphasis on the enduring, often glorifying identification of a group of people with a cultural-religious point of reference outside the current country of living. It is this identificational focus which in biblical terms "gathers the dispersed" (Jer. 32, 37–38) and forms their specific collective identity. Prototypically, that is in most, but not all cases, this situation came about by a migration process. More often than not it involves an identificational difference of the diaspora group in contrast with the society's dominant cultural and religious norms

> and orientations. This difference, a cultural-religious identification bound to a region and culture outside the current country of residence, constitutes an important aspect of the fundamental tripolar interrelatedness of diaspora group, country of origin and country of residence. (Baumann, 327)

For "country of origin," I am substituting here the synchronic connection with other groups in other "countries" with shared cultural practice, whether originating from a single point of origin diachronically or not.

41. Resianne Fontaine, "'Happy Is He Whose Children Are Boys': Abraham Ibn Daud and Avicenna on Evil," *The Arabic, Hebrew and Latin Reception of Avicenna's Metaphysics*, ed. Dag Nikolaus Hasse and Amos Bertolacci, Scientia Graeco-Arabica 7 (Berlin: De Gruyter, 2012) 160.

42. "For a specific example, in a history of black internationalism in France between the world wars, diaspora points not just to the encounter in Marseille between the Senegalese radical Lamine Senghor and the Jamaican novelist Claude McKay, but also to the collaboration in the French Communist Party between Senghor and the Vietnamese radical Nguyen Ai Quoc, later better known as Ho Chi Minh" (Edwards, "The Uses of Diaspora," 64).

43. Cf. "Doubleness as I am conceptualizing it is less a 'both/and' and more a 'neither just this/nor just that.' My attempt here is to conceive doubleness negatively, to explode the positive and equilibristic constructions of diaspora around the desire for belonging ideally to two or more places or cultures. That 'doubleness' is often laced with nostalgia, filial piety, and credulity. It is hardly a space within which a salutary rhetoric of suspicion about official narratives of nation, or about race, gender, sexuality, or class can flourish" (Samir Dayal, "Diaspora and Double Consciousness," *Journal of the Midwest Modern Language Association* 29.1 [1996]: 47).

44.

תלמוד בבלי מסכת גיטין דף נז עמוד ב

אמר רב יהודה אמר רב, מאי דכתיב: על נהרות בבל שם ישבנו גם בכינו בזכרנו את ציון? מלמד, שהראהו הקדוש ברוך הוא לדוד חורבן בית ראשון וחורבן בית שני; חורבן בית ראשון, שנאמר: על נהרות בבל שם ישבנו גם בכינו; בית שני, דכתיב: זכור ה' לבני אדום את יום ירושלים האומרים ערו ערו עד היסוד בה. אמר רב יהודה אמר שמואל, ואיתימא רבי אמי, ואמרי לה במתניתא תנא: מעשה בד' מאות ילדים וילדות שנשבו לקלון, הרגישו בעצמן למה הן מתבקשים, אמרו: אם אנו טובעין בים אנו באין לחיי העולם הבא? דרש להן הגדול שבהן: אמר ה' מבשן אשיב אשיב ממצולות ים, מבשן אשיב - מבין שיני אריה אשיב, ממצולות ים - אלו שטובעין בים; כיון ששמעו ילדות כך, קפצו כולן ונפלו לתוך הים. נשאו ילדים ק"ו בעצמן ואמרו: מה הללו שדרכן לכך - כך, אנו שאין דרכנו לכך - על אחת כמה וכמה! אף הם קפצו לתוך הים. ועליהם הכתוב אומר: כי עליך הורגנו כל היום נחשבנו כצאן טבחה.

See also G. Cohen, "The Story of the Four Captives," 78.

45. G. Cohen, "The Story of the Four Captives," 85.

46. It is a sign of the times in which he was writing more than anything, but it is nonetheless telling that Cohen, while remarking on differences between Ibn Daud and his sources, did not, it seems, see fit to remark on the gendered differences.

47. I owe this point to a comment of Tal Ilan's.

48. It has been suggested to me that the shift from a story in which boys and girls die to one in which only a woman dies has more to do with changes in sexual mores than anything else. While this comment is not entirely inapposite, I would suggest that 1) There is less surety that such a shift in sexual mores from one in which one can imagine desire for boys and women to one where only desire for women is imaginable has taken place; medieval Jewish poetry is rife with poems about desire for boys; 2) Even if such a shift had taken place, here we are representing depraved desire in any case; and 3) Even, again, if such a shift had taken place, it is still enormously significant that Ibn Daud chose to tell the story and to tell it in the way he did.

49. Cf. "We are left with more or less explicit metaphors of the 'fathers of Négritude' that frame its birth as a special kind of immaculate conception" (Brent Hayes Edwards, *The Practice of Diaspora: Literature, Translation, and the Rise of Black Internationalism* [Cambridge, Mass.: Harvard University Press, 2003] 121). Here, once again, I quite disagree with Tsefatman, who insists that there must have been a whole story of his marriage in his new home and that it was to a local woman—"certainly from one of the honored families of the community (as is fitting for a hero)" (Tsefatman, 89).

50. I am grateful to Dina Stein for these reflections.

51. Safran, 83–84.

52. Brubaker, 2.

53. "The approach that I have been following (in tandem with Paul Gilroy, *The Black Atlantic: Modernity and Double Consciousness* [Cambridge, Mass.: Harvard University Press, 1993]) insists on the routing of diaspora discourses in specific maps/histories. Diaspora subjects are, thus, distinct versions of modern, transnational, intercultural experience. Thus historicized, diaspora cannot become a master trope or 'figure' for modern, complex, or positional identities, crosscut and displaced by race, sex, gender, class, and culture" (Clifford, 319). I am happily in tandem with Clifford and Gilroy.

54. Baumann, 325.

55. Cf. the elegant and compellingly nuanced account in Clifford, 306.

56. R. Cohen, 21.

57. Ibid., 22.

58. Ibid., 21. On the one hand, it would seem that here he is relying on Baumann, who writes: “Fundamentally, the term took on spiritual and soteriological meanings, pointing to the ‘gathering of the scattered’ by God’s grace at the end of time. ‘Diaspora’ turns out to be an integral part of a pattern constituted by the fourfold course of sin or disobedience, scattering and exile as punishment, repentance, and finally return and gathering” (Baumann, 317). It seems that Cohen has misread Baumann. What Baumann says is that “diaspora,” scattering, is one part of the process, not that it is a “catch-all” for the whole pattern. On the other hand, Baumann makes the point that this is a purely theological, soteriological notion that has nothing to do with emigration and the possibilities of return. The same point is made, even more clearly, by Tromp, who writes: “Therefore, the basic idea is that the dispersed are the ones who are to be gathered by God (who has himself dispersed them). Consequently, the term says little about the dispersed themselves, or how they would or should experience their situation; all emphasis is on the acts of God.” Even more astonishingly, Tromp goes on to let us know: “What is more, the word διασπορά is not used at all to describe the situation of Jews not living in Judea, not even, with one or two exceptions, for the Jews in the Babylonian exile.” Finally, “The almost complete absence of the term and the use of the concept in non-biblical literature rather suggests that it simply was not part of the current theological and historical interpretation of the Jewish existence outside Judea” (Tromp, all cites, 23). The upshot is that our term “diaspora” in the sense (broadly speaking) in which it is used is *not* a native Jewish term for their own experience, except in the narrow theological sense and bears little or no implication for describing what *we* call the Jewish diaspora or theorizing diaspora tout court from that experience.

59. Baumann, 316. Cohen’s lack of attention to detail is frequently startling: Where on earth does he get the idea that synagogues originated in “earnest discussion groups at the homes of charismatic figures like Jeremiah and Ezekiel”? In the same context, he simply assumes, without question, the accuracy of the suggestion of some scholars that the Torah was codified in Babylonia and that circumcision and the dietary laws all stem from Ezra’s period (R. Cohen, 23). Similarly, Arthur Koestler’s thesis that the Ashkenazi Jews are simply the descendants of Khazar converts is baldly asserted as fact, leading to the claim that “the Turkic Khazars are a wholly different people from the Semitic Sephardim.” I would have no difficulty with such a conclusion were it well established by significant historical arguments—indeed, it would only support my notion of diaspora as a synchronic descriptor, not a diachronic one—but, alas, it isn’t. Koestler’s argument has not been by and large accepted, and not only by “hopping mad Zionists.” No matter for Cohen (R. Cohen, 31).

In his zeal to "supersede" Jewish tradition, Cohen supersedes all truth, completely ignoring the vitality of the Jewish communities of Palestine before and after the destruction of the Temple, dismissing them all as "apocalyptic dreamers, messianic claimants, zealots, revolutionaries and mystics" (R. Cohen, 23), vaunting the Babylonian Talmud as the only important creative Jewish work accomplished in this period and thus ignoring the Mishna (on which, of course, the Talmud is based), the Palestinian Talmud, all the midrashim, and more. One hopes that it is ignorance and not some more mortal sin that motivates this cavalier lack of interest in simple historical fact. In this vale of ignorance, he cheerfully ascribes to Pascal one of Augustine's most well-known and vital ideas, namely, that the Jews should be protected as a living witness to the truth of the Gospel (R. Cohen, 25). He furthermore delivers himself of the pronouncement that Jews were better treated in all Protestant countries than in Catholic ones, that there was no serious anti-Jewish activity until the Crusades, that Jews were very well off throughout the Muslim world, etc.

Cohen expresses a pious wish that "readers will have been patient with my elucidation of Jewish history" (R. Cohen, 34). I dare confess that I have no patience with his obfuscation of Jewish history (except insofar as it demonstrates the need for a book such as this one).

60. Baumann, 317.

61. R. Cohen, 22.

62. See Steven Goldsmith, *Unbuilding Jerusalem: Apocalypse and Romantic Representation* (Ithaca, N.Y.: Cornell University Press, 1993) 61 ff.

63. R. Cohen, 35.

64. For an analysis of this usage with respect to Jews and diaspora studies, see Jonathan Boyarin, in Jonathan Boyarin and Daniel Boyarin, 14.

65. Ibid., 13.

66. Amnon Raz-Krakotzkin, "Exile Within Sovereignty: Toward a Critique of the 'Negation of Exile' in Israeli Culture," *Theory and Criticism: An Israeli Forum* 4 (autumn 1993): 23–56, in Hebrew; English summary, 184–86.

67. Cf. "The accepted risk [of the term "diaspora," DB] is that the term's analytic focus 'fluctuates.' Like Pan-African, it is open to ideological appropriation in a wide variety of political projects, from anticolonial activism to what has long been called 'Black Zionism'—articulations of diaspora that collapse the term into versions of nationalism or racial essentialism" (Edwards, "The Uses of Diaspora," 54).

68. Ibid., 60.

69. Ibid., 46.

70. Tölölyan, 10.

71. My claim is that his description of the Parsis' situation in India and that of Flemish-speaking Walloons is much closer to the situation of the Jews of Babylonia

than his own prescriptive account of the "ideal type" of diaspora—that, allegedly, of the Jews. Truth be told, in spite of Safran's very sympathetic comments about the Palestinians, his account of diaspora is a product of Zionist ideology and not close historical observation of Jewish cultural practice.

72. Cf. Safran's further statement:

> The diaspora of the Parsis is in several respects comparable to that of the Jews: its members have been held together by a common religion, and they have engaged in commerce and the free professions, have been pioneers in industrial innovation, and have performed various useful services to the ruling class. Like the Jews, the Parsis have been loyal to the government. But unlike the Jews, they are not widely dispersed but concentrated in a single area—the Bombay region of India. Moreover, they have no myth of return to their original homeland, Iran, whence they emigrated in the eighth century. The weakness of the Parsis' "homeland" consciousness can be attributed in part to the caste system of India and the relatively tolerant attitudes of Hinduism, both of which made for a greater acceptance of social and ethnocultural segmentation and made Parsis feel less "exceptional" (Safran, 89).

CHAPTER 2

1. Dimitrovsky, "Do the Jews Have a Middle Ages?," 259.

2. Moulie Vidas, "The Bavli's Discussion of Genealogy in Qiddushin IV," *Antiquity in Antiquity: Jewish and Christian Pasts in the Greco-Roman World*, ed. Gregg Gardner and Kevin L. Osterloh, Texts and Studies in Ancient Judaism (Tübingen: Mohr Siebeck, 2008) 326.

3. Benjamin Manasseh Lewin, ed., *Iggeret Rav Sherira Ga'on*, by Sherira Ben Ḥanina (Haifa, 1921) 72–73, in Hebrew.

4. Geonim (also transliterated "gaonim") were the presidents of the two great Babylonian talmudic academies of Sura and Pumbedita, in the Abbasid caliphate, and were the generally accepted spiritual leaders of the Jewish community worldwide from the eighth until the early eleventh century.

5.

כמה דברים מסיעין: נחלת הורים זכות אבות (=אבותיו הגאונים של רב שרירא הכותב) ואף המקום [. . .] שהשכינה שגלתה לבבל מסיעת שנא': למענכם שלחתי בבלה (יש' מג, יד) ופרשו חכמים: חביבין ישראל שכל מקום שגלו השכינה עמהם. ועתה בבבל היא, והיא במקום [. . .] עמדה על כנה ככת': הוי ציון המלטי יושבת [בת ב]בל (זכ' ב, יא). הלא [תלמוד מעידכם] בבל היכא [. . .] שריא שכינה? רב אמ' בכנישתא דהוצל, וש' אמ' בכנישתא בשף ותיב‹!› [בנה]רדעא (מגילה כט.) ולא

תימא הכא ולא תימא הכא אלא אי[מ]א זמנין הכא וזמנין התם [. . .]הם ובה [=בבבל] קביעת
הישיבה לסיוע השכינה [. . .] מברכין [. . .] תמיד אף בכנסת יחזקאל הנביא ודניאל איש חמודות
ועזרא הסופר [וברוך] בן נריה ושאר חכמי התלמוד זכרונם כלם לברכה.

S. (Solomon) Schechter, ed., *Saadyana: Geniza Fragments of Writings of R. Saadya Gaon and Others* (Cambridge: Deighton and Bell, 1903) 123; Samuel Poznánski, *Schechter's Saadyana* (Frankfurt am Main: J. Kauffmann, 1904) 5.

See also:

והראו לו כנישתא דשב ויתיב, ושלוש חומותיה מאבנים וחומת מערבית על נהר פרת וכל החומה אין
לה לא אבן ולא לבינה אלא הכל מעפר שהביא עמו יכניה. ואין גג לאותו בית הכנסת כי הכל חרב
ואמרו לו היהודים שבלילה רואין עמוד אש יוצא משם והולך עד קבר ברוזק שכתבנו לעיל (עמ' 12).
שם, עמ' 17.

I owe these references to my friend Prof. Elḥanan Reiner.

6. Schechter conjectured that the author of the letter was Rabbi Shmuel ben Hofni (d. 1034), the last gaon of Sura (Schechter, 121). This attribution is not proven.

7. For discussion and further bibliography, see Elḥanan Reiner, "'Knesset,' 'Bet Haknesset,' and Holy Place," manuscript submitted for publication (Jerusalem, 2013) nn. 52–54, in Hebrew.

8. "I pause to define tradents. This is both necessary and important because it is a word used by scholars in connection with biblical textual criticism, but it is not found even in unabridged dictionaries. It refers to someone who studies or preserves tradition. The old term for such a person was traditionist, but this was too often confused with traditionalist, that is, one who wants to make the present look like the past. Tradents, on the other hand, examine and process traditions for their own time. Thus, all scribes, translators, commentators, midrashists and even preachers are tradents" (James A. Sanders, "'Spinning' the Bible," http://fontes.lstc.edu/~rklein/Documents/spinningbible.htm).

9. Reiner, "'Knesset,' 'Bet Haknesset,' and Holy Place."

10.

תלמוד בבלי מסכת כתובות דף קיא עמוד א
אמר רב יהודה: כל הדר בבבל - כאילו דר בארץ ישראל, שנאמר: הוי ציון המלטי יושבת בת בבל

11. Richard Marienstras, "On the Notion of Diaspora," *Minority Peoples in the Age of Nation-States*, ed. Gérard Chaliand, trans. Tony Berrett (London: Pluto, 1989) 120.

12. R. Cohen, 4.

13. Ibid., 4 (emphasis original). Thus even when Cohen contests (rightly) the overly negative representation of diaspora on the part of Safran, he does so only

after the fact, recognizing some positive effects of diasporic existence without contesting the traumatic nature of that existence or of its origins (R. Cohen, 7). Fascinatingly, Marienstras distinguishes between "diaspora," which "implies voluntary and free migration," and "exile," which "implies that the home territory has fallen under domination, that the migrations and settlements were forced" (Marienstras, 120). This brings out his further contention that "the notion of diaspora is at once both objective and subjective," but, one might be tempted to remark, much more subjective than objective (Marienstras, 125).

14. See also Steven Vertovec, "Three Meanings of 'Diaspora,' Exemplified Among South Asian Religions," *Diaspora* 6.3 (1997): 293.

15. Robin Cohen's account of the biblical text and the return from Babylonia is tendentious in the extreme (R. Cohen, 23–24), as is his tarring of Christians who refer to Palestine as the Holy Land as "desecularizing Israel and doggedly continuing the 2,000-year-old tradition of deterritorializing the Jews" (R. Cohen, 26). The same space can be configured differently in the *imaginaries* of different groups without one canceling the other. If I refer to the place where the Temple once stood as the Temple Mount, I do not intend to dispute Muslim claims to it as *ḥaram asharif*. I leave it to G-d to sort out what will be there at the eschaton.

16. Isaiah M. Gafni, "Babylonian Rabbinic Culture," *Cultures of the Jews: A New History*, ed. David Biale (New York: Schocken, 2002) 226.

17. As pointed out correctly by Gafni, *Land, Center and Diaspora*, 36 n. 27, this is surely the correct reading and not Rabbi Eli'ezer. This Rabbi El'azar, of Babylonian origin, went to Palestine to study with Rabbi Yoḥanan and ended up his successor.

18. For this as the correct reading here, see Saul Lieberman, *Greek in Jewish Palestine: Studies in the Life and Manners of Jewish Palestine in the II–IV Centuries* CE (New York: Jewish Theological Seminary, 1942) 141, and not Ḥanina, as in the vulgate.

19. For the topos of Roman clemency toward Jews and Jewish brutality, see Josephus, *War* 1.11.

20. Lieberman, 140.

21. See discussion of this passage in Gafni, *Land, Center and Diaspora*, 31–33.

22.

תלמוד בבלי מסכת עבודה זרה דף י עמוד ב

קטיעה בר שלום מאי הוי דההוא קיסרא דהוה סני ליהודאי, אמר להו לחשיבי דמלכותא: מי שעלה לו נימא ברגלו, יקטענה ויחיה או יניחנה ויצטער? אמרו לו: יקטענה ויחיה. אמר להו קטיעה בר שלום: חדא, דלא יכלת להו לכולהו, דכתיב: כי כארבע רוחות השמים פרשתי אתכם, מאי קאמר? אלימא דבדרתהון בד' רוחות, האי כארבע רוחות, לארבע רוחות מבעי ליה! אלא כשם שא"א לעולם בלא רוחות, כך א"א לעולם בלא ישראל; ועוד, קרו לך מלכותא קטיעה. א"ל: מימר שפיר קאמרת, מיהו כל דזכי מלכא שדו ליה לקמוניא חלילא. כד הוה נקטין ליה ואזלין, אמרה ליה ההיא

מטרוניתא: ווי ליה לאילפא דאזלא בלא מכסא! נפל על רישא דעורלתיה קטעה, אמר: יהבית מכסי חלפית ועברית. כי קא שדו ליה, אמר: כל נכסאי לר"ע וחביריו.

23. For a similar analogy between surgery and political execution with an analogous argument against the "amputation," see Josephus, *War* 1.507.

24. Michael Riffaterre, *Text Production*, trans. Terese Lyons (New York: Columbia University Press, 1983).

25. Zvi Septimus, "Ambivalent Artistry: The Effects of the Bavli's Unifying Use of Language on Its Local and Global Readers" (diss., University of California at Berkeley, 2011).

26. Gafni, *Land, Center and Diaspora*, 33.

27. Cf. the entirely different formulation of this in Unnik, 55: "Lietzmann hatte Recht, als er schrieb: 'Das Talmudjudentum hat seine griechisch redende Schwester getötet, ihre Stätte zerstört und den Pflug darüber geführt.'" It would be equally just to claim, I suppose, that it was the Church that murdered diaspora Judentum by absorbing it.

28. According to the Tosefta (Bava Kama 7.3), it was Rabbi Yoḥanan ben Zakkai, centuries earlier than our Rabbi Yoḥanan, who made this statement. See discussion apud Gafni, *Land, Center and Diaspora*, 63. Gafni argues that notions like these were confined to the earlier strata of rabbinic literature, "up to and including the Bar-Kochba war (132–35)." For my purpose here, this doesn't matter, since when the Babylonian Talmud quotes the view, it is "canonical" for them, simultaneous with everything else in the text. Nonetheless, from the historical point of view, Gafni's demonstration of a big shift among Palestinian Rabbis after the revolt is compelling and important.

29. See Jeffrey Rubenstein, "Addressing the Attributes of the Land of Israel: An Analysis of Bavli Ketubot 110b–112a," in Hebrew, with English summary, *Center and Diaspora: The Land of Israel and the Diaspora in the Second Temple, Mishna and Talmud Periods*, in Hebrew, ed. Isaiah M. Gafni (Jerusalem: Merkaz Zalman Shazar le-Toldot Yisrael, 2004) 159–88, discussed further below.

30. Gafni, "Babylonian Rabbinic Culture," 224. See also the illuminating pages in Gafni on the identification of biblical sites with local late antique Babylonian ones and the cultural role of these identifications. Ibid., 228–30.

31. Robert Brody, "Pirqoy Ben Baboy and the History of Internal Polemics in Judaism," *Jewish Culture in Muslim Lands and Cairo Geniza Studies*, ed. Mordechai A. Friedman (Tel Aviv: Tel Aviv University Press, 2003) 3:7–31, in Hebrew.

32. On Pirkoi, see also Gafni, *Land, Center and Diaspora*, 96–97, and, esp., Brody, "Pirqoy Ben Baboy."

33. Dimitrovsky, "Do the Jews Have a Middle Ages?," 263. On this point, see also Fishman, 45.

34. Note that Babylonia was not a term used by the Sasanians to indicate a province, although the Jews continued its usage. Naming the local place with its Hebrew name and refusing its current local name manifests the people as diasporic. For the fourth-century Ammianus Marcellinus, all this area was simply called Assyria in his time. "But in all Assyria, there are many cities, among which Apamia, formerly called Mesene, and Teredon, Apollonia and Vologessia, and many similar ones are conspicuous. But these three are especially magnificent and widely known: Babylon, whose walls Semiramis built with bitumen (for the ancient king Belus built the citadel); and Ctesiphon, which Vardanes founded long ago; and later king Pacorus strengthened it with additional inhabitants and with walls, gave it a Greek name, and made it the crowning ornament of Persia. And finally there is Seleucia, the splendid work of Seleucis Nicator" (R. Garrett Bainbridge, "Ammianus Marcellinus: Description of the 18 Provinces of Sasanian Empire," 5, http://www.humanities.uci.edu/sasanika/pdf/AMMIANUS%20MARCELLINUS%20Province%20of%20Sasanian%20Iran.pdf).

Virtually all the places mentioned in this paragraph are in the locale in which the "Babylonian" Rabbis flourished. It seems that Ammianus was misled by the Iranian name for the province, Āsōristān, into rendering it Assyria and not Babylonia (George Widengren, "A-SO-RISTA-N: Name of the Sasanian Province of Babylonia," *Encyclopaedia Iranica* [New York: Encyclopaedia Iranica Foundation, 1987] 2:785–86). See also such later Jewish usages as Sefarad (Spain), Tzarefat (France), Ashkenaz (Germany), and, most fascinating, Canaan (Bohemia). In all these instances, the local Jews simply planted the Bible over their locales, bringing those locales into the Bible, thus accepting and denying at the same time their emplacement in that place.

35. Richard Kalmin, *Jewish Babylonia Between Persia and Roman Palestine* (Oxford: Oxford University Press, 2006) vii.

36. It would be more precise to say, of course, one of the languages of the Jews of Palestine, since Jews in the period spoke and wrote Aramaic and Greek, as well. Jesus, it would seem, expressed himself in Aramaic. The literature on this topic is legion; see, e.g., Robert H. Gundry, "The Language Milieu of First-Century Palestine: Its Bearing on the Authenticity of the Gospel Tradition," *Journal of Biblical Literature* 83.4 (December 1964): 404–8.

37. Kalmin, *Jewish Babylonia*, ix.

38. Following interpretation of Qorban Ha'edah, ad loc.

39. I want to thank Tal Hever-Chybowski for reminding me of this text.

40. Teshuvot HaRiva"sh, no. 376.

41. As brilliantly shown by Gafni, *Land, Center and Diaspora*, 116.

42. This is the Babylonian form of the Palestinian Ḥananiah.

43.

תלמוד בבלי מסכת ברכות דף סג עמוד א

אמר רב ספרא, רבי אבהו הוה משתעי: כשירד חנינא בן אחי רבי יהושע לגולה היה מעבר שנים וקובע חדשים בחוצה לארץ. שגרו אחריו שני תלמידי חכמים רבי יוסי בן כיפר ובן בנו של זכריה בן קבוטל. כיון שראה אותם, אמר להם: למה באתם? אמרו ליה: ללמוד תורה באנו. הכריז [עליהם]: אנשים הללו גדולי הדור הם, ואבותיהם שמשו בבית המקדש, כאותה ששנינו: זכריה בן קבוטל אומר: הרבה פעמים קריתי לפניו בספר דניאל. התחיל הוא מטמא והם מטהרים, הוא אוסר והם מתירים. הכריז עליהם: אנשים הללו של שוא הם, של תהו הם. אמרו לו: כבר בנית - ואי אתה יכול לסתור, כבר גדרת - ואי אתה יכול לפרוץ. אמר להם: מפני מה אני מטמא ואתם מטהרים, אני אוסר ואתם מתירים? - אמרו לו: מפני שאתה מעבר שנים וקובע חדשים בחוץ לארץ. אמר להם: והלא עקיבא בן יוסף היה מעבר שנים וקובע חדשים בחוץ לארץ? - אמרו לו: הנח רבי עקיבא, שלא הניח כמותו בארץ ישראל. אמר להם: אף אני לא הנחתי כמותי בארץ ישראל. - אמרו לו: גדיים שהנחת נעשו תישים בעלי קרנים, והם שגרונו אצלך, וכן אמרו לנו: לכו ואמרו לו בשמנו: אם שומע - מוטב, ואם לאו - יהא בנדוי.ואמרו לאחינו שבגולה: אם שומעין - מוטב, ואם לאו - יעלו להר, אחיה יבנה מזבח, חנניה ינגן בכנור, ויכפרו כולם ויאמרו: אין להם חלק באלהי ישראל. מיד געו כל העם בבכיה ואמרו: חס ושלום! יש לנו חלק באלהי ישראל. וכל כך למה? - משום שנאמר כי מציון תצא תורה ודבר ה' מירושלים. בשלמא הוא מטהר והם מטמאין - לחומרא, אלא הוא מטמא והם מטהרין, היכי הוי? והא תניא: חכם שטמא - אין חברו רשאי לטהר, אסר - אין חברו רשאי להתיר! - קסברי: כי היכי דלא נגררו בתריה.

44. For discussion of this phrase and the fact that it was always used by Babylonian "traitors" who had left Babylonia to live in Palestine, see Rubenstein, 162–63.

45. Ibid., 164.

CHAPTER 3

1. Dimitrovsky, "Do the Jews Have a Middle Ages?," 264 (translation mine).

2. Anthony Grafton, *Worlds Made by Words: Scholarship and Community in the Modern West* (Cambridge, Mass.: Harvard University Press, 2009).

3.

תלמוד בבלי מסכת שבת דף קח עמוד ב

תני רבי יהודה בר חביבא: אין מולחין צנון וביצה בשבת. רב חזקיה משמיה דאביי אמר: צנון - אסור, וביצה - מותרת. אמר רב נחמן: מריש הוה מלחנא פוגלא, אמינא: אפסודי קא מפסידנא ליה, דאמר שמואל: פוגלא חורפי מעלי. כיון דשמענא להא, דכי אתא עולא ואמר: במערבא מלחי כישרי כישרי, ממלח - לא מלחנא, טבולי - ודאי מטבילנא. תני רבי יהודה בר חביבא: אתרוג צנון וביצה, אילמלא קליפתן החיצונה - אינן יוצאין מבני מעיים לעולם.

כי אתא רב דימי אמר: מעולם לא טבע גברא בימא דסדום. אמר רב יוסף: הפוכה סדום, והפוכה מילה; גברא הוא דלא טבע, כשורא טבע? אמר ליה אביי: לא מיבעיא קאמר, לא מבעיא כשורא - דאפילו בכל מימות שבעולם לא טבע, אלא אפילו גברא דטבע בכל מימות שבעולם - בימא דסדום

לא טבע. למאי נפקא מינה? - כי הא, דרבין הוה שקיל ואזיל אחוריה דרבי ירמיה אגודא דימא דסדום, אמר ליה: מהו למימשי מהני מיא בשבת? - אמר ליה: שפיר דמי. מהו למימץ ולמיפתח? אמר ליה: זו לא שמעתי, כיוצא בה שמעתי; דאמר רבי זירא, זימנין אמר לה משמיה דרב מתנה וזימנין אמר לה משמיה דמר עוקבא, ותרווייהו משמיה דאבוה דשמואל ולוי אמרין, חד אמר: יין בתוך העין - אסור, על גב העין - מותר, וחד אמר: רוק תפל, [אפילו] על גב העין - אסור.

4. Edwards, *The Practice of Diaspora*.

5. Kosher/ not kosher has to do with whether we may eat of the food; pure/impure has to do with whether a person is in a state fit to go into the Temple. There are things that one may touch that render the body impure and thus not fit to go into the Temple, but kosher food that is impure may be eaten (this point is key to understanding the Gospels). On the distinction between pure/impure and kosher/not kosher and its relevance to the Gospel, see Daniel Boyarin, *The Jewish Gospels: The Story of the Jewish Christ* (New York: New Press, 2012) 112–17.

6. The word *tirta* is obscure.

7.

תלמוד בבלי מסכת חולין דף קכד עמוד א

תני'. עור שיש עליו כזית בשר, הנוגע בציב היוצא ממנו, ובשערה שכנגדו - טמא. היו עליו כשני חצאי זיתים - מטמא במשא ולא במגע, דברי רבי ישמעאל, רבי עקיבא אומר: לא במגע ולא במשא, ומודה רבי עקיבא בשני חצאי זיתים שתחבן בקיסם והסיטן שהוא טמא, ומפני מה רבי עקיבא מטהר בעור - מפני שהעור מבטלן.

גמ'. אמר עולא אמר רבי יוחנן: לא שנו אלא פלטתו חיה, אבל פלטתו סכין - בטיל. אמר ליה רב נחמן לעולא: אמר רבי יוחנן אפילו כתרטא? אמר ליה: אין; ואפילו כנפיא? א"ל: אין, א"ל: האלהים! אם אמר לי רבי יוחנן מפומיה לא צייתנא ליה! כי סליק רב אושעיא אשכחיה ליה לרבי אמי, אמרה לשמעתיה קמיה: הכי אמר עולא והכי אהדר ליה רב נחמן, א"ל: ומשום דרב נחמן חתניה דבי נשיאה הוא, מזלזל בשמעתיה דר' יוחנן? זמנין אשכחיה דיתיב וקאמר לה אסיפא: היו עליו שני חצאי זיתים - מטמאים במשא ולא במגע דברי ר' ישמעאל, ר"ע אומר: לא במגע ולא במשא א"ר יוחנן: לא שנו אלא פלטתו חיה, אבל פלטתו סכין - בטיל, א"ל: מר אסיפא מתני להָ? א"ל: אין, ואלא עולא ארישא אמרה ניהליכו? א"ל: אין; א"ל: האלהים! אי אמר לי יהושע בן נון משמיה לא צייתנא ליה! כי אתא רבין וכל נחותי אמרוה ארישא.

8. This point, Rav Naḥman's "class," will reappear in the next section of this chapter as well.

9. It is perhaps a very telling detail that he mentions Joshua and not Moses here, for, as Elḥanan Reiner has been showing lately, Joshua had a special place in the religious imaginary of the Galilean Jews. Elḥanan Reiner, "From Joshua to Jesus: The Transformation of a Biblical Story to a Local Myth: A Chapter in the Religious Life of the Galilean Jew," *Sharing the Sacred: Religious Contacts and Conflicts in the Holy Land*, ed. Guy G. Stroumsa and Arieh Kofsky (Jerusalem: Yad Izḥak Ben-Zvi, 1998) 223–71.

10. Gilroy.

11. See Jonathan Boyarin, "Reconsidering Diaspora," unpublished paper (2013).

12. After decades of virtual neglect following World War II, the Babylonian-ness—i.e., Iranian-ness—of the Babylonian Talmud is being rediscovered and illuminated. It should be noted that after that war, Jewish rabbinics scholars mostly neglected Christian literature as well, beginning widely to investigate those connections again at about the same time that the Iranian background of the Bavli was being interrogated. The reason that the latter has not been studied as widely is not ideological so much as owing to the much greater difficulties (difficulty of Middle Persian, lack of texts contemporary with the Talmud, lack of good editions of those texts, and the more narrow focus of the Persian texts) attendant on such research versus work on Jewish texts and patristic literature.

13. For an excellent introduction to this field, see Yaakov Elman, "Middle Persian Culture and Babylonian Sages: Accommodation and Resistance in the Shaping of Rabbinic Legal Tradition," *The Cambridge Companion to the Talmud and Rabbinic Literature*, ed. Charlotte Elisheva Fonrobert and Martin S. Jaffee, Cambridge Companions to Religion (Cambridge: Cambridge University Press, 2007) 165–97. In addition to other scholars whom I might not have occasion to mention in this short account, I would note especially the work of Reuven Kipperwasser and Dan Shapira, "Irano-Talmudica I—the Three-Legged Ass and 'Ridya' in B. Ta'anith: Some Observations About Mythic Hydrology in the Babylonian Talmud and in Ancient Iran," *AJS Review* 32 (2008): 101–16, and, in Hebrew, Reuven Kipperwasser and Dan Shapira, "Massa'ot shel Rabbah Bar Bar Hannah [The Journeys of Rabbah Bar Bar Hannah]," *Sifrut Umered*, ed. Ariel Hirschfeld, Hannan Hever, and Joshua Levinson (Jerusalem: Hebrew University, 2008) 215–41. For a much more extensive and concise survey of the field, including nearly a full bibliographical listing of Elman's myriad publications in this area of research, see notes in Shai Secunda, "Talmudic Text and Iranian Context: On the Development of Two Talmudic Narratives," *AJS Review* 33 (2009): 45–69. See also the history of research in this field in Shai Secunda, *The Iranian Talmud: Reading the Bavli in Its Sasanian Context*, Divinations: Rereading Late Ancient Religion (Philadelphia: University of Pennsylvania Press, 2013) 10–14.

14. Secunda, *The Iranian Talmud*.

15. W. E. B. Du Bois, *The Souls of Black Folk: Authoritative Text, Contexts, Criticism*, ed. Henry Louis Gates Jr. and Terri Hume Oliver (New York: W. W. Norton, 1999).

16. Gafni, *Land, Center and Diaspora*, 41.

17. Ibid., 61.

18. Ibid., 73.

19. Ibid., 74.

20. Ibid., 77.

21. See, on this topic, the beautiful Hebrew lecture of my great teacher, Prof. Saul Lieberman, OBM, at http://www.ybz.org.il/_Uploads/dbsAttachedFiles/Article_17.9.pdf, accessed February 5, 2015.

22. Christine Hayes, *Between the Babylonian and Palestinian Talmuds* (Oxford: Oxford University Press, 1997), with the caveat that the Palestinian Talmud quotes only relatively early Babylonians.

23. As Gafni almost suggests, the narrative of their weeping may be an artificial literary (and ideological) construct of the editor of the Sifri (c. fourth century). Gafni's argument that much of the focus on Palestine in the post–Bar Kochba period is a kind of propaganda designed to keep the Land from becoming denuded of Jews in the wake of that disaster seems most plausible. Gafni, *Land, Center and Diaspora*, 66–67.

24. Berakhot 43a and 46b.

25. Geoffrey Herman, "Table Etiquette and Persian Culture in the Babylonian Talmud," *Zion* 77.2 (2012): 165, in Hebrew.

26. Secunda, *The Iranian Talmud*.

27. Tal Hever-Chybowski, personal communication, January 2013.

28. Kalmin, *Jewish Babylonia*, 103. While my interests in this book are quite different from Kalmin's in his, he is explicitly and heavily invested in learning history from these sources, and I am not. While I have in certain details come to different conclusions from him, I have learned much from his work.

29. Ibid., 108–9.

30. Ibid., 110–14.

31. Ibid., 116.

32. Ibid., 109, emphasis added.

33. Lacking this perspective leads Kalmin here and there into real misjudgment in my opinion. Thus he writes: "In Palestine, the story obviously would have had relevance as a protest against the emperor cult, which many scholars believe to have been the most important and widely diffused cult in the Roman Empire in late antiquity. To the extent that the story is Babylonian, it may be valuable contemporary evidence of an emperor cult in Sasanian Persia as well" (ibid., 118). But we hardly need come to such a conclusion, since worship of the Roman emperor within the Roman Empire would be of just as much concern, I am arguing, to the Rabbis of Babylonia. Moreover, Kalmin partly contradicts his own conclusion here when he emphasizes later on in the book the intense concern that the Babylonian Rabbis had for their Palestinian compatriots (ibid., 137), a concern that was not matched, he argues, by a similar one on the part of the Palestinian Rabbis, who were, nonetheless, content to quote many dicta of the Babylonian Rabbis.

34. Ibid., 120.

35. Cf. the somewhat different critical take on Kalmin in Secunda, *The Iranian Talmud*, 141–42.

36. Joseph Naveh and Shaul Shaked, *Magic Spells and Formulae: Aramaic Incantations of Late Antiquity* (Jerusalem: Magnes, 1993) 21.

37. Daniel Boyarin, "Hellenism in Rabbinic Babylonia," *The Cambridge Companion to the Talmud and Rabbinic Literature*, ed. Charlotte Elisheva Fonrobert and Martin S. Jaffee (Cambridge: Cambridge University Press, 2007) 336–63.

38. Flood, 9.

39. Gafni, "Babylonian Rabbinic Culture," 239.

40. Adam H. Becker, *The Fear of God and the Beginning of Wisdom: The School of Nisibis and Christian Scholastic Culture in Late Antique Mesopotamia*, Divinations: Rereading Late Ancient Religion (Philadelphia: University of Pennsylvania Press, 2006) 5.

41. There are prefigurations of such ideas in the apocalyptic literature of the Second Temple, as well—notably, in 4 Ezra in such passages as 4 Ezra 4:35–36, "Did not the souls of the righteous in their treasuries ask about these matters, saying, 'How long are we to remain here? And when will come the harvest of our reward?' And Jeremiel the archangel answered them and said, 'When the number of those like yourselves is completed'"; 4 Ezra 4:40–42a, "He answered me and said, 'Go and ask a woman who is with child if, when her nine months have been completed, her womb can keep the child within her any longer.' 'No, my lord,' I said, 'it cannot.' He said to me, 'In Sheol the treasury of the souls are like the womb.'" See Matthias Henze, *Jewish Apocalypticism in Late First Century Israel: Reading 'Second Baruch' in Context*, Texts and Studies in Ancient Judaism (Tübingen: Mohr Siebeck, 2011) chap. 4. See also John J. Collins, *The Apocalyptic Imagination: An Introduction to the Jewish Matrix of Christianity* (New York: Crossroad, 1984) 195–224.

42. Richard Paul Vaggione, *Eunomius of Cyzicus and the Nicene Revolution*, Oxford Early Christian Studies (Oxford: Oxford University Press, 2000) 119–20.

43. Any analysis I can provide here is owing to Vaggione's erudition and to the diligence of my research assistant, Ruth Haber, who tracked down and provided for me copies of every one of the many sources that Vaggione cites; perusal of his footnotes will show that erudition and diligence are formidable.

44. Moreno Morani, ed., *Nemesii Emeseni de Natura Hominis* (Leipzig: B. G. Teubner, 1987) 30. For "the Truth" as a name for Platonism, see Plotinus, Ennead II 9, 6.10–12. This term is being used as late as the fifteenth century among Jews as well. For the Aristotle, which does indeed break with Plato, see Aristotle, *On the Soul* 2.2.414a.

45. Harry Sysling, *Teḥiyyat ha-Metim: The Resurrection of the Dead in the Palestinian Targums of the Pentateuch and Parallel Traditions in Classical Rabbinic Literature* (Tübingen: J. C. B. Mohr [Paul Siebeck], 1996) 194, who points out as well

the signal differences between the rabbinic and the apocalyptic versions of the idea. I am grateful to Ishay Rosen-Zvi for calling this reference to my attention.

46. Vaggione, 119 n. 255.

47. Clement of Rome, "Recognitions of Clement," *The Writings of Tatian and Theophilus, and the Clementine Recognitions* (Edinburgh: T. & T. Clark, 1867) 121.

48. Vaggione, 120 n. 257.

49. Albert I. Baumgarten, "Literary Evidence for Jewish Christianity in the Galilee," *The Galilee in Late Antiquity*, ed. Lee I. Levine (New York: Jewish Theological Seminary, 1992) 39–50.

50. Ephraim E. Urbach, *The Sages: Their Concepts and Beliefs*, trans. Israel Abrahams (Jerusalem: Magnes, 1975) 1:237 .

51. Sysling, 207.

52. Adam H. Becker, "Beyond the Spatial and Temporal *Limes*: Questioning the 'Parting of the Ways' Outside the Roman Empire," *The Ways That Never Parted Jews and Christians in Late Antiquity and the Early Middle Ages*, ed. idem and Annette Yoshiko Reed (Tübingen: Mohr Siebeck, 2003) 373–92.

53. Shaye J. D. Cohen, "Patriarchs and Scholarchs," Proceedings of the American Academy of Jewish Research 48 (1981): 85. See also Becker, *The Fear of God*, 14–15. Further, Abraham Wasserstein has adumbrated such a result: "The Jews were as susceptible to the lure and influence of Hellenism as their gentile neighbours. This is no less true of the Aramaic-speaking Jews in Palestine and Babylonia than of those of their coreligionists who, living in Asia Minor or in Egypt, or in Greek-speaking cities in Palestine and Syria, had either adopted Greek speech or inherited it from their forebears." Abraham Wasserstein, "Greek Language and Philosophy in the Early Rabbinic Academies," *Jewish Education and Learning Published in Honour of Dr. David Patterson on the Occasion of His Seventieth Birthday* (Chur, Switzerland: Harwood Academic, 1994).

I thank Shamma Boyarin for bringing this essay to my attention.

54. Kalmin, *Jewish Babylonia*, 174.

55. For a recent and very effective challenge to the notion of influence in the study of late ancient Jewish cultures, see Michael L. Satlow, "Beyond Influence: Towards a New Historiographic Paradigm," *Jewish Literatures and Cultures: Context and Intertext*, ed. Anita Norich and Yaron Z. Eliav, Brown Judaic Studies 349 (Providence, R.I.: Brown Judaic Studies, 2008) 37–53.

56. For discussions of this story, see Catherine Hezser, "The Slave of a Scholar Is Like a Scholar," *Creation and Composition: The Contribution of the Bavli Redactors to the Aggadah*, ed. J. L. Rubenstein (Tübingen: Mohr Siebeck, 2005) 181–200; Richard Kalmin, *The Sage in Jewish Society of Late Antiquity* (New York: Routledge, 1999) 52–57; Jacob Neusner, *A History of the Jews in Babylonia: [Vol.] 2, The*

Early Sasanian Period (Leiden: Brill, 1966) 65–67, 142–45; Vidas; and Barry Wimpfheimer, *Narrating the Law: A Poetics of Talmudic Legal Stories*, Divinations: Rereading Late Ancient Religion (Philadelphia: University of Pennsylvania Press, 2011) 147–63. See also the remarkable reading of this narrative in Septimus, from which this bibliography was compiled as well.

57. I have given the text here as it is found in Ms. Oxford Opp. 248.

58. Elman, 173–75. See also summary in Secunda, *The Iranian Talmud*, 5.

59. Septimus gets this right, in my view.

60. כדאמרי אינשי, "as folk say," is the usual term for introducing a proverb into the Talmud as well. See, esp., Galit Hasan-Rokem, "An Almost Invisible Presence: Multilingual Puns in Rabbinic Literature," *The Cambridge Companion to the Talmud and Rabbinic Literature*, ed. Charlotte Elisheva Fonrobert and Martin S. Jaffee, Cambridge Companions to Religion (Cambridge: Cambridge University Press, 2007) 222–40.

61. Dayal, 46.

62. "Doch schon lange vorher hatte der Hellenismus eine 'kosmopolitische' Dimension und das griechische Denken eine 'universalistische' Form angenommen, deren spezifisch 'logische' Strukturen in das Denken des östlichen Mittelmeerraums einzudringen begann" (Christina von Braun, "Virtuelle Genealogien," *Hybrid Jewish Identities* [2013], forthcoming)

63. Said, 186.

64. Herman writes of quite a different story in the Talmud: "This story, at any rate, sets its task to object to the admiration of Persian culture and its preference over Jewish culture" (Herman, "Table Etiquette and Persian Culture in the Babylonian Talmud," 175).

65. Rubenstein.

66. Secunda, *The Iranian Talmud*, 15.

67. Ibid., 15–16 and 155, n. 45.

68. Ibid., 131.

69. The powerfully diachronic orientation offered by Secunda is manifested, e.g., in his statement that "the possibility of these historical interactions will set the stage for the central claim of the book, namely that one can perceive the Bavli's interaction with its Persian cultural and literary context not only in talmudic anecdotes concerning Sasanian people, materials, and institutions, but also—especially—in the textual shifts in and resonances of seemingly insular rabbinic texts that transmit and reconfigure earlier, often Palestinian traditions" (Secunda, *The Iranian Talmud*, 133).

70. This, despite his correct recognition that "parallels include Palestinian citations of Babylonian amoraim and stories set in Babylonia, both of which are either unattested in the Bavli, or appear in different versions" (ibid., 15).

71. Correcting with all the mss. from Rav Ashi, a much later figure.

72. Ms. Florence II-I-7, the oldest manuscript of Berakhot.

73. In two other important manuscripts, the final statement beginning here "rather" is cited in the name of the Babylonian Abbaye.

74. PT Berakhot chap. 8, 12c (according to Venice edition).

75. As Robert Bonfil has remarked: "[A] different ruler did not form a barrier and the slowness of transportation was not perceived, as we would think living in the jet-age" (Bonfil, "Myth, Rhetoric, History," 101).

76. For a case in which one could argue that the contact with the Mazdeans led to greater emphasis on a celebration with fire, see Geoffrey Herman, "Religious Transformation Between East and West: Hanukkah in the Babylonian Talmud and Zoroastrianism," *"Trading Religions": Religions Formation, Transformation and Cross-Cultural Exchange Between East and West*, ed. P. Wick and V. Rabens (Leiden: Brill, 2012). Herman refers to the attempts of the priests to suppress this Jewish observance, suggesting to me the possibility that it was provocative to the Persian priests. For further support for my suggestion that the Babylonian Rabbis were, at least occasionally, under pressure owing to similarity or dissimilarity from Mazdean practice, see Moshe Beer, "Notes on Three Edicts Against the Jews of Babylonia in the Third Century CE," *Irano-Judaica* 1 (1982): 25–37, in Hebrew; Robert Brody, "Judaism in the Sasanian Empire: A Case Study in Religious Coexistence," *Irano-Judaica* 2 (1990): 52–62.

77. Gafni, *Land, Center and Diaspora*, 116.

78. Von Braun. I wish to thank Prof. von Braun for sending me her paper prior to publication and for sharing the wonderful turn of phrase with me.

CHAPTER 4

1. Dimitrovsky, "Do the Jews Have a Middle Ages?," 265.

2. Bari, the last Byzantine outpost, fell to the Normans in 1071.

3. Fontaine, 160.

4. Abramson.

5. For a wonderful analogy, see Gilroy, 33.

6. Fishman, 123.

7. Fishman effectively dismisses on chronological grounds the suggestion of Israel Ta-Shma that the early Jewish settlers in the Rhineland brought with them sophisticated legal culture when they came from Lucca (ibid., 23).

8. This provides an answer to the argument for an Ashkenazi origin for these methods on the grounds that for the Sefardim, the primary purpose of study was to

arrive at the law by simple and direct means. Once Naḥmanides brings Sefarad into the intellectual world of the Tosafists, things shift dramatically, and we have just as natural an environment for the development of *pilpul* as there had been allegedly in France and Germany (cf. Hayyim Zalman Dimitrovsky, "By Way of *Pilpul*," *Salo Wittmayer Baron: Jubilee Volume on the Occasion of His Eightieth Birthday*, Saul Lieberman [ed.] and associate ed. Arthur Hyman [Jerusalem: American Academy for Jewish Research, 1974] 3:160–61, in Hebrew). If we assume that the *pilpul* came from Ashkenaz to R"Y Kanpanton, it would be difficult to understand why he ignored the Tosafot (the central text for Ashkenazi *pilpul*) and concentrated solely on Naḥmanides.

9. Hayyim Zalman Dimitrovsky, "The Academy of R'I Berav in Safed," *Sefunot* 7 (1962): 80, in Hebrew.

10. Yitzḥak Kanpanton, *Darkhe hatalmud*, ed. Y. Sh. Langeh (Jerusalem: Y. Sh. Langeh, 1980 or 1981).

11. In previous publications, I have confused these two dates in my memory and given 1493 for Kanpanton's death. In a translation of *Darkhe hatalmud* that I am preparing, Javier Castana will provide a full historical and biographical introduction to R"Y Kanpanton. For the very meager biographical knowledge we have had before Castana's research, see Abraham David, "On R. Isaac Canpanton, One of the Great Fifteenth-Century Scholars," *Kiryat Sefer* 52 (1965–66): 324–26, in Hebrew.

12. Kanpanton, 57.

13. It can also develop the sense of what is implied in the language, as in the following usage of Shmuel Ibn Sid: "A mishna or baraita from which he could have objected using that which is explicit in the language, but instead used that which is implicit" (*Kelale Shmuel* [Venice: 1622], n.p.), i.e., in the more usual terminology of talmudic scholarship, the *diyyuq*. Indeed, *beko'aḥ* and *bepo'al* are used in both Hebrew and Arabic (*bi-l-kuwwa bi-l-fi'l*) logical writings to mean "explicit" and "implicit."

14. Moses Maimonides, Israel Efros, Moses ibn Tibbon, and Ahitub ben Isaac, *Maimonides' Treatise on Logic (Makalah Fi-Sina at al-Mantik): The Original Arabic and Three Hebrew Translations*, ed. and trans. Israel Efros (New York: American Academy for Jewish Research, 1938) 59. This passage is practically a quotation from Al-Farabi's introduction to logic, as has been pointed out by Efros.

15. Abraham ben Isaac ben Judah ben Samuel Shalom (d. 1492), *Hakdamat ha-Ma'atik: Ha-She'elot veha-Teshuvot al Mevo Ma'amarot u-Melitsah Lehe-Hakham Marsilyo* (Leipzig: Defus shel Friedrikh Foster, 1859) 7.

16. Dimitrovsky, "By Way of *Pilpul*," 124; Daniel Boyarin, "Studies in the Talmudic Commentary of the Spanish Exiles, I; The Method of Diaeresis," *Sefunot*, n.s., 2 (1983): 183–84, in Hebrew.

17. Emmanuel Hasefaradi, *Meharrerei Nemerim* (Venice, 1509) 16 (erroneously paginated 19).

18. Simon Shalem, "The Hermeneutic Method of Rabbi Joseph Taitazak and His Circle," *Sefunot* 11 (1962–1963): 121, in Hebrew.

19. *Sefer Alilot Devarim* (Venice: 1468), n.p.

20. See also the text cited in Dimitrovsky, "By Way of *Pilpul*," 138 n. 142, as well as the example cited at D. Boyarin, "Method of Diaeresis," 182, from Maharam Schiff.

21. Galit Hasan-Rokem, "Ökotyp," *Encyclopädie des Märchens*, vol. 10 (Berlin: Walter de Gruyter, 2000) 258–63.

22. In an appendix to this chapter, I offer two extended analyses of the semantic and logical formations of other Kanpantonian methods, connecting them back with Arabic logic and forward up to Ashkenazi *pilpul*.

23. Itamar Even-Zohar, "Factors and Dependencies in Culture: A Revised Outline for Polysystem Culture Research," *Canadian Review of Comparative Literature* 24.1 (1997): 15–34.

24. Drory, 184.

25. Ibid., 7.

26. Ibid., 194–95.

27. Ibid., 198.

28. Ibid., 206.

29. Kanpanton, 26.

30. Dimitrovsky, "By Way of *Pilpul*," 111–12.

31. Ibid., 118.

32. Ibid., 119 n. 34.

33. Ibid., 122 n. 53.

34. See discussion in D. Boyarin, "Method of Diaeresis," 181 n. 77.

35. Ibid. Together with my colleague Dr. Islam Dayeh at the Wissenschaftskolleg zu Berlin, I am currently preparing an expanded English version of this paper, in which we plan to explore much more thoroughly the Arabic background of this usage.

36. J. van Ess, "The Logical Structure of Islamic Theology," *Logic in Classical Islamic Culture*, ed. G. E. von Grunebaum (Wiesbaden: O. Harrassowitz, 1970) 14–40. For the Jewish usage (ninth century), see Georges Vajda, "La Finalité del la création de l'homme selon un théologien Juif du ixe Siècle," *Oriens* 15 (1952): 61–85.

37. Moses Maimonides, *The Guide for the Perplexed*, trans. M. Friedländer (New York: Dover, 1956) 2.1.

38. For the nonce, an example of this operation translated into English can be found in Daniel Boyarin, "Moslem, Christian, and Jewish Cultural Interaction in Sefardic Talmudic Interpretation," *Journal of Rabbinic Judaism* 5.1 (2002): 24–26. It

will immediately be seen by anyone familiar with ancient and medieval philosophy that this analytic procedure applied to the Talmud is identical to that used since Plato.

39. Dimitrovsky, "By Way of *Pilpul*," 119 n. 34.

40. For a comparison between actual examples of a Sefardic *ḥaluqah* and an Ashkenazi *ḥilluq*, see D. Boyarin, "Method of Diaeresis," 181–82, as well as the forthcoming article of Boyarin and Dayeh.

41. Dimitrovsky, "The Academy of R'I Berav in Safed," 80.

42. For a masterful study of the history of the yeshiva at Safed at this time, including the itinerancy of its sages, see ibid., on which much of the next two paragraphs is based.

43. Ibid., 77–93.

44. Ibid., 77.

45. Ibid., 96.

46. Dimitrovsky, "By Way of *Pilpul*," 162–64.

47. For a much fuller account of this mode of talmudic learning than I can give here, see Dimitrovsky, "The Academy of R'I Berav in Safed," followed by Daniel Boyarin, *Sephardi Speculation* (Jerusalem: Mekhon Ben-Tsevi, 1989), in Hebrew.

48. Dimitrovsky, "By Way of *Pilpul*," 164.

49. Dimitrovsky, "Do the Jews Have a Middle Ages?," 265.

50. Cf. Dimitrovsky, "By Way of *Pilpul*," 132, and esp. 135–36, claiming the precise opposite; and again, 160–61.

51. Edwards, *The Practice of Diaspora*, 122.

52. Daniel Boyarin and Jonathan Boyarin, "Diaspora: Generation and the Ground of Jewish Identity," *Critical Inquiry* 19.4 (summer 1993): 693–725.

53. J. Boyarin and D. Boyarin. I would like to say that part of my effort in this book is to respond once again from another perspective to Clifford's call for "diaspora discourses [that] retain a connection with specific bodies, historical experiences of displacement," and not "slide into equivalence with disaggregated, positional, performed identities in general" (Clifford, 324).

54. Floya Anthias, "Evaluating 'Diaspora': Beyond Ethnicity," *Sociology* 32.3 (1998): 557–80.

55. Clifford, 313.

56. Ibid., 314.

57. Ibid., 323.

58. For Rabbi Ya'akov Pollack, together with his *pilpul*, as a founding figure for the new Eastern European diaspora via his move from Prague to Kraków, see Max Weinreich, *History of the Yiddish Language*, trans. Shlomo Noble, Yale Language Series (New Haven, Conn.: Yale University Press, 2008) 4. If my argument above is

acceptable, he was the vehicle of the transport of a version of the Sefardic scholastic mode of Talmud study to the East of Europe.

59. Naomi Seidman, *A Marriage Made in Heaven: The Sexual Politics of Hebrew and Yiddish*, Contraversions (Berkeley: University of California Press, 1997).

60. Weinreich, 184.

61. Ibid., 208.

62. Ibid., 202. I have modified here and there the great Shlomo Noble's overly faithful rendering. On Noble, see Jonathan Boyarin, *A Storyteller's Worlds: The Education of Shlomo Noble in Europe and America* (New York: Holmes, 1994).

63. Weinreich, 207.

64. One further way of thinking this is via the move from textuality to performance, performed by Gilroy, 36. See also Galit Hasan-Rokem, *Tales of the Neighborhood: Jewish Narrative Dialogues in Late Antiquity* (Berkeley: University of Californa Press, 2003) 10–12.

65. Eliyahu Stern, *The Genius: Elijah of Vilna and the Making of Modern Judaism* (New Haven, Conn.: Yale University Press, 2013) 37–53.

66. Among the other achievements of Stern's work is his clear argument that the Jews of eighteenth-century Eastern Europe were *not* minorities in their separate locales, but in many places, including Vilna, they constituted the majority of the population, such that "Vilna's Jews were more aware of the differences among Maskilim, Hasidim, and Mitnagdim, and were less engaged in the happenings of the minorities that lived among them, such as Catholics and Protestants" (ibid., 71).

67. This is why I have found that the notion of *translatio studii* is not quite adequate for describing the role of talmudic learning in Jewish diasporic history and life.

68. Kanpanton, 26. All translations mine.

69. Cf. F. W. Zimmerman, ed., *Al-Farabi's Commentary and Short Treatise on Aristotle's De Interpretatione*, trans. F. W. Zimmermann, Classical and Medieval Logic Texts (London: Oxford University Press, 1981) lxi.

70. For this usage, see also Apollonius Dyscolus, Synt. 22.21, ἔξωθεν ὑπακούεσθαι: "understand what one has in mind without it needing to be expressed" (Apollonius Dyscolus, *Apollonii Dyscoli Quae Supersunt*, Grammatici Graeci [Lipsiae: Teubner, 1878–1910]).

71. Zimmerman, lxii.

72. Ibid., cxxxi.

73. Cf. Dimitrovsky, "By Way of *Pilpul*," 133–35. I am not convinced that all uses of *baḥuẓ* mean the same: some examples cited there seem quite different—e.g., to refer simply to a passage cited from another location, which is not the same as what would be understood without a text. These probably represent misunderstandings

of the original term on the order of the later Ḥatam Sofer's misunderstanding of *pilpul* tout court as being about comparison of texts rather than intensive examination of the logic of the single text. My lamented teacher's masterpiece of intellectual history has been a lamp unto my feet throughout this section of my presentation. Even when I have offered supplements to his conclusions, it is only by virtue of what I have learned from him and his work.

Bibliography

Abramson, Shraga. *Ba-Merkazim uvatefutsot bi-Tekufat ha-Ge'onim*. Jerusalem: Mosad Harav Kook, 1965.

Anthias, Floya. "Evaluating 'Diaspora': Beyond Ethnicity." *Sociology* 32.3 (1998): 557–80.

Apollonius Dyscolus. *Apollonii Dyscoli Quae Supersunt*. Grammatici Graeci. Lipsiae: Teubner, 1878–1910.

Bainbridge, R. Garrett. "Ammianus Marcellinus: Description of the 18 Provinces of Sasanian Empire." http://www.humanities.uci.edu/sasanika/pdf/AMMIANUS%20MARCELLINUS%20Province%20of%20Sasanian%20Iran.pdf.

Baumann, Martin. "Diaspora: Genealogies of Semantics and Transcultural Comparison." *Numen* 47.3 (2000): 313–37.

Baumgarten, Albert I. "Literary Evidence for Jewish Christianity in the Galilee." *The Galilee in Late Antiquity*, ed. Lee I. Levine. New York: Jewish Theological Seminary, 1992. 39–50.

Becker, Adam H. "Beyond the Spatial and Temporal *Limes*: Questioning the 'Parting of the Ways' Outside the Roman Empire." *The Ways That Never Parted: Jews and Christians in Late Antiquity and the Early Middle Ages*, ed. idem and Annette Yoshiko Reed. Tübingen: Mohr Siebeck, 2003. 373–92.

———. *The Fear of God and the Beginning of Wisdom: The School of Nisibis and Christian Scholastic Culture in Late Antique Mesopotamia*. Divinations: Rereading Late Ancient Religion. Philadelphia: University of Pennsylvania Press, 2006.

Beer, Moshe. "Notes on Three Edicts Against the Jews of Babylonia in the Third Century CE." *Irano-Judaica* 1 (1982): 25–37. In Hebrew.

Bonfil, Robert. *History and Folklore in a Medieval Jewish Chronicle: The Family Chronicle of Aḥima'az ben Paltiel*. Leiden: Brill, 2009.

———. "Myth, Rhetoric, History? A Study in the Chronicle of Ahima'z." *Culture and Society in Medieval Jewry*, ed. Reuven Bonfil, Menahem Ben-Sasson, and Yosef Hacker. Jerusalem: Merkaz Zalman Shazar le-Toldot Yisrael, 1989. In Hebrew.

Boyarin, Daniel. "Hellenism in Rabbinic Babylonia." *The Cambridge Companion to the Talmud and Rabbinic Literature*, ed. Charlotte Elisheva Fonrobert and Martin S. Jaffee. Cambridge Companions to Religion. Cambridge: Cambridge University Press, 2007. 336–63.

———. *The Jewish Gospels: The Story of the Jewish Christ*. New York: New Press, 2012.

———. "Moslem, Christian, and Jewish Cultural Interaction in Sefardic Talmudic Interpretation." *Journal of Rabbinic Judaism* 5.1 (2002): 1–34.

———. *Sephardi Speculation*. Jerusalem: Mekhon Ben-Tsevi, 1989. In Hebrew.

———. "Studies in the Talmudic Commentary of the Spanish Exiles, I; The Method of Diaeresis." *Sefunot*, n.s., 2 (1983): 165–84. In Hebrew.

Boyarin, Daniel, and Jonathan Boyarin. "Diaspora: Generation and the Ground of Jewish Identity." *Critical Inquiry* 19.4 (summer 1993): 693–725.

Boyarin, Jonathan. "Reconsidering Diaspora." Unpublished paper, 2013.

———. *A Storyteller's Worlds: The Education of Shlomo Noble in Europe and America*. Foreword by Sander L. Gilman. New York: Holmes, 1994.

Boyarin, Jonathan, and Daniel Boyarin. *Powers of Diaspora: Two Essays on the Relevance of Jewish Culture*. Minneapolis: University of Minnesota Press, 2002.

Brody, Robert. "Judaism in the Sasanian Empire: A Case Study in Religious Coexistence." *Irano-Judaica* 2 (1990): 52–62.

———. "Pirqoy Ben Baboy and the History of Internal Polemics in Judaism." *Jewish Culture in Muslim Lands and Cairo Geniza Studies*, ed. Mordechai A. Friedman. Tel Aviv: Tel Aviv University Press, 2003. 3:7–31. In Hebrew.

Brubaker, Rogers. "The 'Diaspora' Diaspora." *Ethnic and Racial Studies* 28.1 (2005): 1–19.

Clement of Rome. "Recognitions of Clement." *The Writings of Tatian and Theophilus, and the Clementine Recognitions*. Edinburgh: T. & T. Clark, 1867. 75–211.

Clifford, James. "Diasporas." *Cultural Anthropology* 9 (August 1994): 302–38.

Cohen, Gerson D. *A Critical Edition with a Translation and Notes of the Book of Tradition (Sefer ha-Qabbalah) by Abraham Ibn Daud*. Judaica Texts and Translations 3. N.p.: Jewish Publication Society of America, 1967.

———. "The Story of the Four Captives." *Proceedings of the American Academy for Jewish Research* 29 (1960–61): 55–131.

Cohen, Robin. *Global Diasporas: An Introduction*. 2nd ed. Global Diasporas. London: Routledge, 2008.

Cohen, Shaye J. D. "Patriarchs and Scholarchs." *Proceedings of the American Academy of Jewish Research* 48 (1981): 57–83.

Cohn, Naftali S. *The Memory of the Temple and the Making of the Rabbis*. Divinations: Rereading Late Ancient Religion. Philadelphia: University of Pennsylvania Press, 2013.

Collins, John J. *The Apocalyptic Imagination: An Introduction to the Jewish Matrix of Christianity*. New York: Crossroad, 1984.

David, Abraham. "On R. Isaac Canpanton, One of the Great Fifteenth-Century Scholars." *Kiryat Sefer* 52 (1965-66): 324–26. In Hebrew.

Dayal, Samir. "Diaspora and Double Consciousness." *Journal of the Midwest Modern Language Association* 29.1 (1996): 46–62.

Dimitrovsky, Hayyim Zalman. "The Academy of R'I Berav in Safed." *Sefunot* 7 (1962): 43–112. In Hebrew.

———. "By Way of *Pilpul*." *Salo Wittmayer Baron: Jubilee Volume on the Occasion of His Eightieth Birthday*, ed. Saul Lieberman and Arthur Hyman. Jerusalem: American Academy for Jewish Research, 1974. 3:111–82. In Hebrew.

———. "Do the Jews Have a Middle Ages?." *Meḥkarim be-Madaʿe ha-Yahadut*, ed. Moshe Bar Asher. Jerusalem: Hebrew University, 1986. 257–65. In Hebrew.

Drory, Rina. *Models and Contacts: Arabic Literature and Its Impact on Medieval Jewish Culture*. Brill's Series in Jewish Studies 25. Leiden: Brill, 2000.

Du Bois, W. E. B. *The Souls of Black Folk*. Ed. Henry Louis Gates Jr. and Terri Hume Oliver. New York: W. W. Norton, 1999.

———. *The World and Africa: An Inquiry into the Part Which Africa Has Played in World History*. New York: International, 1965.

Edwards, Brent Hayes. *The Practice of Diaspora: Literature, Translation, and the Rise of Black Internationalism*. Cambridge, Mass.: Harvard University Press, 2003.

———. "The Uses of Diaspora." *Social Text* 19.1 (spring 2001): 45–74.

Elman, Yaakov. "Middle Persian Culture and Babylonian Sages: Accommodation and Resistance in the Shaping of Rabbinic Legal Tradition." *The Cambridge Companion to the Talmud and Rabbinic Literature*, ed. Charlotte Elisheva Fonrobert and Martin S. Jaffee. Cambridge Companions to Religion. Cambridge: Cambridge University Press, 2007. 165–97.

Fishman, Talya. *Becoming the People of the Talmud: Oral Torah as Written Tradition in Medieval Jewish Cultures*. Jewish Culture and Contexts. Philadelphia: University of Pennsylvania Press, 2011.

Flood, Finbarr B. *Objects of Translation: Material Culture and Medieval "Hindu-Muslim" Encounter*. Princeton, N.J.: Princeton University Press, 2009.

Fontaine, Resianne. "'Happy Is He Whose Children Are Boys': Abraham Ibn Daud and Avicenna on Evil." *The Arabic, Hebrew and Latin Reception of Avicenna's Metaphysics*, ed. Dag Nikolaus Hasse and Amos Bertolacci. Scientia Graeco-Arabica 7. Berlin: De Gruyter, 2012. 159–75.

Gafni, Isaiah M. "Babylonian Rabbinic Culture." *Cultures of the Jews: A New History*, ed. David Biale. New York: Schocken, 2002. 224–97.

———. "The Babylonian Yeshiva as Reflected in Bava Kama 111a." *Tarbiẓ* 49 (1980): 292–301. In Hebrew; English summary, v–vi.

———. *Land, Center and Diaspora: Jewish Constructs in Late Antiquity*. Sheffield: Sheffield Academic Press, 1997.

Gilroy, Paul. *The Black Atlantic: Modernity and Double Consciousness*. Cambridge, Mass.: Harvard University Press, 1993.

Goldsmith, Steven. *Unbuilding Jerusalem: Apocalypse and Romantic Representation*. Ithaca, N.Y.: Cornell University Press, 1993.

Goodblatt, David M. *Rabbinic Instruction in Sasanian Babylonia*. Studies in Judaism in Late Antiquity 9. Leiden: E. J. Brill, 1975.

Grafton, Anthony. *Worlds Made by Words: Scholarship and Community in the Modern West*. Cambridge, Mass.: Harvard University Press, 2009.

Grossman, Avraham. "The Yeshiva of Eretz Israel: The Literary Output and the Relationship with the Diaspora." *The History of Jerusalem: The Early Muslim Period, 638–1099*, ed. Joshua Prawer and Haggai Ben-Shammai. Jerusalem: Yad Izḥak Ben-Zvi; New York: New York University Press, 1996. 225–69.

Gundry, Robert H. "The Language Milieu of First-Century Palestine: Its Bearing on the Authenticity of the Gospel Tradition." *Journal of Biblical Literature* 83.4 (December 1964): 404–8.

Hasan-Rokem, Galit. "An Almost Invisible Presence: Multilingual Puns in Rabbinic Literature." *The Cambridge Companion to the Talmud and Rabbinic Literature*, ed. Charlotte Elisheva Fonrobert and Martin S. Jaffee. Cambridge Companions to Religion. Cambridge: Cambridge University Press, 2007. 222–40.

Hasefaradi, Emmanuel. *Meharrerei Nemerim*. Venice, 1509.

Hayes, Christine. *Between the Babylonian and Palestinian Talmuds*. Oxford: Oxford University Press, 1997.

Helmreich, Stefan. "Kinship, Nation, and Paul Gilroy's Concept of Diaspora." *Diaspora* 2.2 (1992): 243–49.

Henze, Matthias. *Jewish Apocalypticism in Late First Century Israel: Reading "Second Baruch" in Context*. Texts and Studies in Ancient Judaism. Tübingen: Mohr Siebeck, 2011.

Herman, Geoffrey. "Religious Transformation Between East and West: Hanukkah in the Babylonian Talmud and Zoroastrianism." *"Trading Religions": Religions Formation, Transformation and Cross-Cultural Exchange Between East and West*, ed. P. Wick and V. Rabens. Leiden: Brill, 2012.

———. "Table Etiquette and Persian Culture in the Babylonian Talmud." *Zion* 77.2 (2012): 149–88. In Hebrew.

Hezser, Catherine. "The Slave of a Scholar Is Like a Scholar." *Creation and Composition: The Contribution of the Bavli Redactors to the Aggadah*, ed. J. L. Rubenstein. Tübingen: Mohr Siebeck, 2005. 181–200.

Kalmin, Richard. *Jewish Babylonia Between Persia and Roman Palestine*. Oxford: Oxford University Press, 2006.

———. *The Sage in Jewish Society of Late Antiquity*. New York: Routledge, 1999.

Kanpanton, Yitzḥak. *Darkhe hatalmud*. Ed. Y. Sh. Langeh. Jerusalem: Y. Sh. Langeh, 1980 or 1981.

Kipperwasser, Reuven, and Dan Shapira. "Irano-Talmudica I—the Three-Legged Ass and 'Ridya' in B. Ta'anith: Some Observations About Mythic Hydrology in the Babylonian Talmud and in Ancient Iran." *AJS Review* 32 (2008): 101–16.

———. "Massa'ot shel Rabbah Bar Bar Hannah [The Journeys of Rabbah Bar Bar Hannah]." *Sifrut Umered*, ed. Ariel Hirschfeld, Hannan Hever, and Joshua Levinson. Jerusalem: Hebrew University, 2008. 215–41.

Lewin, Benjamin Manasseh, ed. *Iggeret Rav Sherira Ga'on*, by Sherira Ben Ḥanina. Haifa, 1921. In Hebrew.

Lieberman, Saul. *Greek in Jewish Palestine: Studies in the Life and Manners of Jewish Palestine in the II–IV Centuries* CE. New York: Jewish Theological Seminary, 1942.

Maimonides, Moses. *The Guide for the Perplexed*. Trans. M. Friedländer. New York: Dover, 1956.

Maimonides, Moses, Israel Efros, Moses ibn Tibbon, and Ahitub ben Isaac. *Maimonides' Treatise on Logic (Makalah Fi-Sina at al-Mantik): The Original Arabic and Three Hebrew Translations*. Ed. and trans. Israel Efros. New York: American Academy for Jewish Research, 1938.

Marienstras, Richard. "On the Notion of Diaspora." *Minority Peoples in the Age of Nation-States*, ed. Gérard Chaliand, trans. Tony Berrett. London: Pluto, 1989. 119–25.

Naveh, Joseph, and Shaul Shaked. *Magic Spells and Formulae: Aramaic Incantations of Late Antiquity*. Jerusalem: Magnes, 1993.

Nemesius, Moreno Morani, ed. *Nemesii Emeseni de Natura Hominis*. Leipzig: B. G. Teubner, 1987.

Neusner, Jacob. *A History of the Jews in Babylonia: [Vol.] 2, The Early Sasanian Period*. Leiden: Brill, 1966.

Poznánski, Samuel. *Schechter's Saadyana*. Frankfurt am Main: J. Kauffmann, 1904.

Raz-Krakotzkin, Amnon. "Exile Within Sovereignty: Toward a Critique of the 'Negation of Exile' in Israeli Culture." *Theory and Criticism: An Israeli Forum* 4 (autumn 1993): 23–56; English summary, 184–86.

Reiner, Elḥanan. "From Joshua to Jesus: The Transformation of a Biblical Story to a Local Myth: A Chapter in the Religious Life of the Galilean Jew." *Sharing the Sacred: Religious Contacts and Conflicts in the Holy Land*, ed. Guy G. Stroumsa and Arieh Kofsky. Jerusalem: Yad Izḥak Ben-Zvi, 1998. 223–71.

———. "'Knesset,' 'Bet Haknesset,' and Holy Place." Manuscript submitted for publication. Jerusalem, 2013. In Hebrew.

Riffaterre, Michael. *Text Production*. Trans. Terese Lyons. New York: Columbia University Press, 1983.

Rubenstein, Jeffrey. "Addressing the Attributes of the Land of Israel: An Analysis of Bavli Ketubot 110b–112a." *Center and Diaspora: The Land of Israel and the Diaspora in the Second Temple, Mishna and Talmud Periods*, ed. Isaiah M. Gafni. Jerusalem: Merkaz Zalman Shazar le-Toldot Yisrael, 2004. 159–88. In Hebrew, with English summary.

Safran, William. "Diasporas in Modern Societies: Myths of Homeland and Return." *Diaspora* 1 (1991): 83–99.

Said, Edward W. *Reflections on Exile and Other Essays*. Convergences. Cambridge, Mass.: Harvard University Press, 2000.

Satlow, Michael L. "Beyond Influence: Toward a New Historiographic Paradigm." *Jewish Literatures and Cultures: Context and Intertext*, ed. Anita Norich and Yaron Z. Eliav. Brown Judaic Studies 349. Providence, R.I.: Brown Judaic Studies, 2008. 37–53.

Schechter, S. (Solomon), ed. *Saadyana: Geniza Fragments of Writings of R. Saadya Gaon and Others*. Cambridge: Deighton and Bell, 1903.

Scheffer, Gabriel. *Diaspora Politics: At Home Abroad*. Cambridge: Cambridge University Press, 2003.

Schremer, Adiel. "'He Posed Him a Difficulty and Placed Him': A Study in the Evolution of the Text of TB Bava Kama 117a." *Tarbiẓ* 66.3 (April–June 1997): 403–15. In Hebrew; English summary, viii.

Secunda, Shai. *The Iranian Talmud: Reading the Bavli in Its Sasanian Context*. Divinations: Rereading Late Ancient Religion. Philadelphia: University of Pennsylvania Press, 2013.

———. "Talmudic Text and Iranian Context: On the Development of Two Talmudic Narratives." *AJS Review* 33 (2009): 45–69.

Seidman, Naomi. *A Marriage Made in Heaven: The Sexual Politics of Hebrew and Yiddish*. Contraversions. Berkeley: University of California Press, 1997.

Septimus, Zvi. "Ambivalent Artistry: The Effects of the Bavli's Unifying Use of Language on Its Local and Global Readers." Diss., University of California at Berkeley, 2011.

Shalem, Simon. "The Hermeneutic Method of Rabbi Joseph Taitazak and His Circle." *Sefunot* 11 (1962-63). In Hebrew.

Shalom, Abraham ben Isaac ben Judah ben Samuel. *Hakdamat ha-Ma'atik: Ha-She'elot veha-Teshuvot al Mevo Ma'amarot u-Melitsah lehe-Hakham Marsilyo.* Leipzig: Defus shel Friedrikh Foster, 1859.

Sökefeld, Martin. "Mobilizing in Transnational Space: A Social Movement Approach to the Formation of Diaspora." *Global Networks* 6.3 (2006): 265–84.

Stein, Dina. "Let the 'People' Go: On the 'Folk' and Their 'Lore' as Tropes in the Reconstruction of Rabbinic Culture." *Prooftexts* 29 (2009): 206–41.

Stern, Eliyahu. *The Genius: Elijah of Vilna and the Making of Modern Judaism*. New Haven, Conn.: Yale University Press, 2013.

Sysling, Harry. *Teḥiyyat ha-Metim: The Resurrection of the Dead in the Palestinian Targums of the Pentateuch and Parallel Traditions in Classical Rabbinic Literature.* Tübingen: J. C. B. Mohr (Paul Siebeck), 1996.

Theophilus of Antioch. *Ad Autolycum*. Ed. and trans. Robert M. Grant. Oxford Early Christian Texts. Oxford: Clarendon, 1970.

Tölölyan, Khachig. "Rethinking Diaspora(s): Stateless Power in the Transnational Moment." *Diaspora* 5.1 (1996): 3–36.

Tromp, Johannes. "The Ancient Jewish Diaspora: Some Linguistic and Sociological Observations." *Strangers and Sojourners: Religious Communities in the Diaspora*, ed. Gerrie ter Haar. Leuven: Peeters, 1998. 13–35.

Tsefatman, Sarah. *Rosh ve-Rishon: Yisud Manhigut be-Sifrut Yisra'el.* Jerusalem: Magnes, 2010.

Unnik, Willem Cornelis van. *Das Selbstverständnis der jüdischen Diaspora in der hellenistisch-römischen Zeit.* Ed. Pieter Willem van der Horst. Arbeiten zur Geschichte des antiken Judentums und des Urchristentums. Leiden: Brill, 1993.

Urbach, Ephraim E. *The Sages: Their Concepts and Beliefs*. Trans. Israel Abrahams. 2 vols. Jerusalem: Magnes, 1975.

Vaggione, Richard Paul. *Eunomius of Cyzicus and the Nicene Revolution*. Oxford Early Christian Studies. Oxford: Oxford University Press, 2000.

Vajda, Georges. "La Finalité del la création de l'homme selon un théologien Juif du ixe Siècle." *Oriens* 15 (1952): 61-85

van Ess, Josef. "The Logical Structure of Islamic Theology." *Logic in Classical Islamic Culture*, ed. G. E. von Grunebaum. Wiesbaden: O. Harrassowitz, 1970. 14–40.

Vertovec, Steven. "Three Meanings of 'Diaspora,' Exemplified Among South Asian Religions." *Diaspora* 6.3 (1997): 277–99.

Vidas, Moulie. "The Bavli's Discussion of Genealogy in Qiddushin IV." *Antiquity in Antiquity: Jewish and Christian Pasts in the Greco-Roman World*, ed. Gregg

Gardner and Kevin L. Osterloh. Texts and Studies in Ancient Judaism. Tübingen: Mohr Siebeck, 2008. 285–326.

von Braun, Christina. "Virtuelle Genealogien." *Hybrid Jewish Identities*, 2013. Forthcoming.

Weinreich, Max. *History of the Yiddish Language*. Trans. Shlomo Noble. 2 vols. Yale Language Series. New Haven, Conn.: Yale University Press, 2008.

Widengren, George. "A-SO-RISTA-N: Name of the Sasanian Province of Babylonia." *Encyclopaedia Iranica*. New York: Encyclopaedia Iranica Foundation, 1987. 2:785–86.

Wimpfheimer, Barry. *Narrating the Law: A Poetics of Talmudic Legal Stories*. Divinations: Rereading Late Ancient Religion. Philadelphia: University of Pennsylvania Press, 2011.

Yarden, Dov. *Divan Shmuel HaNagid*. Vol. 5. Jerusalem: Hebrew Union College, 1966.

Zimmerman, F. W., ed. and trans. *Al-Farabi's Commentary and Short Treatise on Aristotle's De Interpretatione*. Classical and Medieval Logic Texts. London: Oxford University Press, 1981.

Index of Names and Subjects

18–19, 132n42; as synchronic state of doubled consciousness and cultural location (trans-local identity), 19–21, 54–55, 65–69, 82, 107, 130–31n36; trauma as not necessary or sufficient condition for, 5, 17, 19, 25
Dimi, Rav, 56
Dimitrovsky, Hayyim Zalman, 5, 8, 97; and the Babylonian Talmud as traveling homeland for medieval Jewry, 16, 54; on early modern Ashkenazi invention of method of *pilpul* and *ḥilluqim*, 110–11, 112; on Pirkoi ben Baboi's controversial supersessionist claim, 46; on the *sebara mibbaḥuẓ*, 123, 152–53n73; and Sefardic learning that traveled to sixteenth-century Ashkenaz, 115–16; and Sefardic learning that traveled to sixteenth-century Safed in Galilee, 115
Dominicus Gundissalinus, 21, 97–98
Drory, Rina, 107–8
Du Bois, W. E. B., 18, 19, 65
Dunaš Ben Labraṭ, 107–8, 109–10

ecotypification, 105, 120
Edwards, Brent Hayes, 18, 31, 59, 132n42, 133n49, 135n67
El'azar, bar Pedat, Rabbi, 42
El'azar, Rabbi, 39, 42–43, 138n17
Elḥanan, R., 11
Eliyahu of Vilna, 120
Elman, Yaakov, 65, 69, 79–80, 83, 95
Eunomius, 74–77
Ezekiel, Prophet, 35, 36
Ezra the Scribe, 35

Al-Farabi, Abū Naṣr Muḥammad ibn Muḥammad, 103, 122
Fishman, Talya, 98, 148n7
Flood, Finbar, 19–21, 72
foundation legends for centers of talmudic learning. *See* Ibn Daud's narrative of the four captives (foundation legend of the major centers of talmudic learning)

Gafni, Isaiah, 66–67, 69, 73, 95–96, 139n28; on late tannaitic story of three Rabbis who wept at border of the Holy Land, 67, 144n23; on positive accounts of the Babylonian exile/scattering outside the Roman Empire, 38–39, 42, 43–44
Garvey, Marcus, 18
gender and diaspora. *See* women's diaspora
The Genius (Stern), 120
geonim (gaonim), 34–36, 136n4
Gilroy, Paul, 30–31, 64, 133n53
Goodblatt, David M., 127n7
Grossman, Avraham, 129n24

Hai Gaon, Rav, 15, 16, 129n24
Hall, Stuart, 30, 31
Halperin, David, 65
ḥaluqah, Sefardic, 111–13; and Ashkenaz *ḥilluqim*, 112–13; and Islamic logicians (the Arabic *kalam*), 111–12; Maimonides' use of, 111–12; Plato and, 111, 150–51n38
Ḥananel, Rabbenu, 11, 16, 24, 129n24
Ḥananiah (the nephew of Rabbi Yehoshua): intercalation of the calendar in Babylon, 48–53, 67, 95–96; story in the Palestinian Talmud, 48–53; story of Ḥanina in the Bavli, 50–53, 95–96; weeping at leaving the Holy Land, 67

Index of Ancient Texts

Acknowledgments

A love song to the Talmud and a threnody for my teacher, this book originated as a set of lectures commissioned and delivered at the University of Pennsylvania under the auspices of the Cross-Cultural Contacts initiative, generously sponsored by the Andrew W. Mellon Foundation. I am thankful for the opportunity to organize decades of thought on this topic under that stimulus and in that venue.

The book was written while I was a most happy fellow at the Wissenschaftskolleg zu Berlin in the academic year 2012–13. I am very grateful to that institution, and especially to its rector, Prof. Luca Giuliani, for providing such a comfortable and stimulating home for my research. I would like to thank Jonathan Boyarin, Shamma Boyarin, Yishai Boyarin, Tal Hever-Chybowski, Amnon Raz-Krakotzkin, and Shai Secunda for reading very early drafts of parts of the book. Parts of Chapters 1 and 2 were presented in earlier avatars at the Institute for Cultural Investigation (Berlin), the Wissenschaftskolleg zu Berlin, the Hochschule für Wissenschaft des Judentums in Heidelberg, the Center for Jewish Studies of the Berlin Universities (when Chapter 2 had the benefit of critical commentary by Prof. Micha Brumlik). Comments made after the first occasion were of particular use and stimulation to me, especially those of Prof. Lorraine Daston and Prof. Joanna Masel. I am grateful to all those venues for providing me with opportunities to receive responses and to improve the chapters. I am further grateful to the following friends who read an early draft of the whole thing and offered many important comments: Jonathan Boyarin, Galit Hasan-Rokem, Derek Krueger, Ishay Rosen-Zvi, and Dina Stein. I am grateful, as well, for the comments of Khachig Tölölyan, who functioned very helpfully as a (non-)anonymous reader for the Press. It would have been a worse book had I not taken any of their advice and, no doubt, a much better one had I been capable of attending to all of it. The usual disclaimers apply.